INTRODUCTION to JAZZ GUITAR

Jane Miller

To access audio visit:
www.halleonard.com/mylibrary

Enter Code
6907-6448-6701-0272

Berklee Press

Editor in Chief: Jonathan Feist
Vice President of Online Learning and Continuing Education: Debbie Cavalier
Assistant Vice President of Operations for Berklee Media: Robert F. Green
Assistant Vice President of Marketing and Recruitment for Berklee Media: Mike King
Dean of Continuing Education: Carin Nuernberg
Editorial Assistants: Reilly Garrett, Emily Jones, Eloise Kelsey, Zoë Lustri
Cover Design: Small Mammoth Design
Cover Photos: Emily Joy Ashman

ISBN 978-0-87639-155-6

1140 Boylston Street
Boston, MA 02215-3693 USA
(617) 747-2146

Visit Berklee Press Online at
www.berkleepress.com

Study with

BERKLEE ONLINE

online.berklee.edu

DISTRIBUTED BY

HAL•LEONARD®
CORPORATION
7777 W. BLUEMOUND RD. P.O. BOX 13819
MILWAUKEE, WISCONSIN 53213

Visit Hal Leonard Online at
www.halleonard.com

Berklee Press, a publishing activity of Berklee College of Music, is a not-for-profit educational publisher.
Available proceeds from the sales of our products are contributed to the scholarship funds of the college.

CONTENTS

ACKNOWLEDGMENTS

For my students.

My office is a mess. The way I figure it, this book will really help neaten things up in there by giving my written exercises and handouts a home. The truth is, I learn so much from my students. Good teachers are challenged to find new analogies, new perspectives, new ways to sharpen the focus on an idea with every lesson, every student. Over time, I've found myself writing things down that work. This book saves me from a whole lot of filing.

I'm grateful to the people that have let me be a writer, and I have tremendous respect for their writing and editing expertise. At *Acoustic Guitar Magazine*: Andrew DuBrock, Dan Apczynski, Dan Gabel, Teja Gerken, Scott Nygaard, Mark Segal Kemp, Greg Cahill. At *Premier Guitar Magazine*: Gayla Drake, Jason Shadrick, and Shawn Hammond. My writer friends Jane Eklund and Clare Innes could talk a dog off a meat truck with their way with words, and I've loved our conversations. Neil Ian MacKillop turned me on to Rudolf Flesch, and so much more, and I will always feel lucky to know him.

Finally, Jonathan Feist has quietly done the necessary mopping up of any messes I made with words and punctuation. He has also shown a deep and quick understanding of the material in this book and has provided just the right direction for me to fine tune its presentation, all with great mutual respect.

INTRODUCTION

I remember the day I "discovered" a C6(9) chord on the guitar. I found it by applying what I knew to be true in theory to the notes on the neck near the C chord that I could already play. My excitement waned only a little when I realized that lots of players had found that voicing before I did. But my sense of discovery has remained intact, and I see no end to the process of finding new ways to play through a chord progression or to improvise a single note line through a tune.

Guitarists of all styles want to improve their playing. Many players feel that learning jazz guitar is beyond their reach and interest, yet they harbor the belief that if they could learn jazz, they would be better players. Just learning music theory can go a long way toward better understanding the enigma of the fretboard. What some may view as jazz techniques are, in fact, just guitar or general musicianship techniques. All players can grow from learning major scales, for example.

These chapters suggest ways to understand the guitar. There are specific examples to practice and commit to memory, and there are chapters that are meant to inspire you to find your own way. The lessons here are for the many guitarists I have met who are stuck at a particular point in their playing. For example, performing singer-songwriters who play guitar will tell me that they want something to play between verses or during an interlude. Players who identify as lead players want to get more familiar with seventh chords and tensions. Players who play mostly rhythm want to be able to take a solo break. Imagine what learning a chord-melody solo could do for the singer-songwriter, what comping a jazz-blues progression with tensions could do for the player with the single-line chops, or what scales and arpeggios could do for the dedicated chord player.

To be sure, this book is for guitarists who aspire to play jazz in its many configurations: as a solo guitarist, in a trio or quartet, accompanying a vocalist or a melody player, or other jazz contexts. But guitarists who already play in any other style will find some valuable crossover material here.

Use this information as you see fit. Become the jazz player that you know you can be armed with the confidence from these lessons to continue your creative search. Become a more intelligent player in your own folk, pop, rock, or blues style, and break through the limits you have reached in your playing. Above all, give thought to the material. It is meant to show you a way to get started. The way to continue is for your creative self to discover through experimenting, listening, thinking, and playing for the joy of making music.

ABOUT THE RECORDINGS

To access the accompanying audio, go to www.halleonard.com/mylibrary and enter the code found on the first page of this book. This will grant you instant access to every example. Examples with accompanying audio are marked with an audio icon, like this one for my tune "Blue Betty." "Blue Betty" is a just-for-fun track to get you in the mood for playing some jazz.

1
"Blue Betty"

Demo tracks are for listening, demonstrating a technique. Play-along tracks are provided for playing in unison with what is heard and seen in the corresponding examples. Backing tracks are accompaniment chords only for the purpose of practicing your own melodies, scales, or improvisations in context.

CHAPTER 1

The Layout

The guitar is an ongoing puzzle to be solved. It can seem like a daunting task to even begin to name the notes on the neck, let alone memorize them. We know the names of the open strings from low to high: E A D G B E. Consider this: every fret is one-half step; two frets make a whole step. That is enough information for you to go on to name every note on the guitar. However, the stretch between the nut and the 22nd fret is a long one if you're navigating without any reference points to help identify the notes. The following diagram shows a way to divide the neck into smaller, more manageable sections.

Reference Points

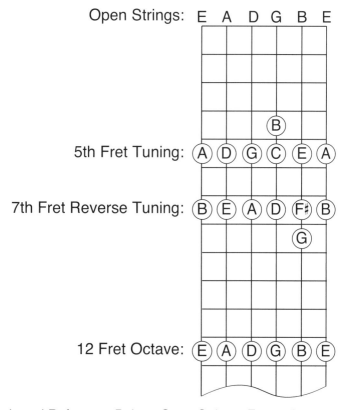

FIG. 1.1. Guitar Fretboard Reference Points. Open Strings, Fret 5, Fret 7, Fret 12 (Octave).

Reference Point 1: Open Strings. E A D G B E. Eat A Darn Good Breakfast Early

Reference Point 2: 5th Fret Tuning. Many of us learn to tune by fingering the note on the 5th fret of the low E to tune the next string, A, and so on, with the exception being at the third string 4th fret to hear the next string, B. If we are tuning to those notes, then it makes good sense to realize and remember that those fretted notes are named the same as the next higher adjacent string. Note that whatever note is on the low E string will be the same note name on the high E string, two octaves higher. The space between the open strings and the 5th fret becomes a nice, small, workable section that is quite manageable.

Reference Point 3: Reverse Octave Tuning. The 7th fret of the A string sounds an octave higher than the open E string. Continue this way across the neck, this time compensating for the different interval between G and B by going up to the 8th fret on the B string to get G. Since B will be found on the 7th fret of the high E string, that is also the name of the note on the low E string, 7th fret, two octaves lower. That leaves only two frets, or a whole step, to work with between the 5th fret reference point and the 7th fret. Pretty doable.

Reference Point 4: 12th Fret Octave. The guitar starts over again. Eat A Darn Good Breakfast Early. The space between frets 7 and 12 is also an easy area to study and learn.

Quick, what's the 9th fret of the G string? Reference point at the 7th fret G string is D. A whole step higher than that is E. Or, if you'd rather, reference point on the 12th fret G string is G. Back up one whole step to F and one half-step to E at the 9th fret.

Major Scale Fingerings (And the Chords Who Love Them)

Jazz guitarists rely in part on scales to create melodies. So do songwriters, composers, and all instrumentalists. Improvising with single-note lines is simply inventing melodies in real time in the context of a song's chord progression. To get started, it is important to learn some fingerings for major scales. You know major scales already: Do Re Mi Fa Sol La Ti Do. You can no doubt sing them by memory. Take a moment here to find a major scale on the guitar.

Did you start on Do? Did you start with your first finger? Did you use any open strings? What key did you play (what note was "Do")? How many octaves did you play?

There are many right answers to these questions. The point here is to put your attention on these options and gain awareness of how you approach playing a scale. To be a fluent improviser, you'll need to be comfortable playing major scales (for starters) all over the neck—in the same key!

Here are seven different places on the guitar where you can play a C major scale.

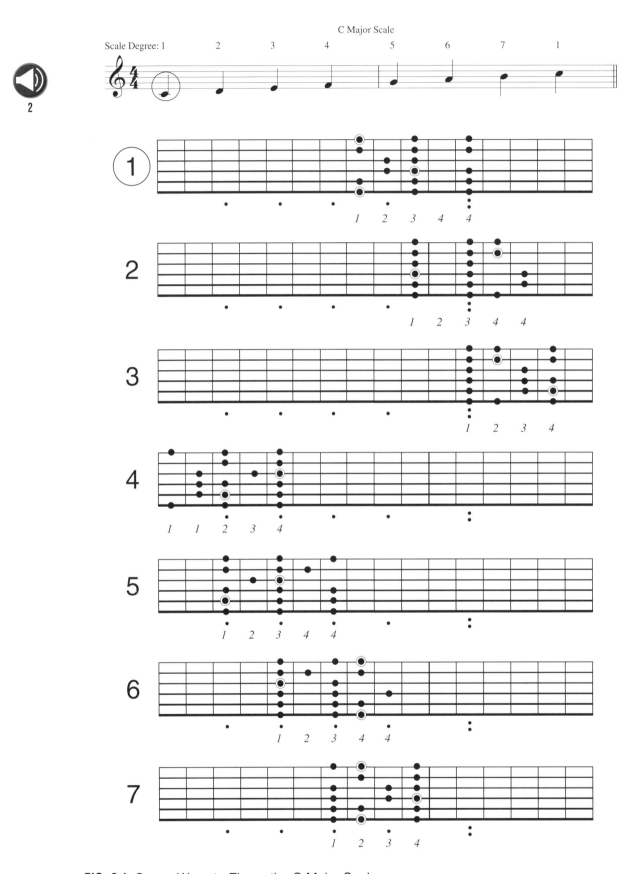

FIG. 2.1. Seven Ways to Finger the C Major Scale

Notice that each scale fingering shown starts on a different scale degree using your first finger as a starting place. The fingerings are named by the scale degree on which they start (1 to 7). "Do" is circled so that you will keep this important reference in your mind's ear. Memorize fingerings 3 and 7 first; there are no finger stretches, and they can be committed to muscle (and mental) memory quickly. For example, fingering 7 is 1 2 4 twice, 1 3 4 twice, 2 4 by itself, and back to 1 2 4. (Whatever is played on the sixth string will also be played on the first string, two octaves higher).

A *position* is a bit of a territorial assignment of your fingers on the frets. In the 5th fret position, fingers 1, 2, 3, and 4 fall on frets 5, 6, 7, and 8, respectively. If needed, your first finger can stretch back to play a note on the 4th fret, and your fourth finger can stretch up to play a note on the 9th fret. Fingers 2 and 3, however, should remain constant on the 6th and 7th frets. That will ensure place keeping as you play through the scale.

Look at scale fingering 6. There is one finger stretch found on the fourth string where your fourth finger reaches up to the 9th fret to play the note B ("Ti"). Be sure to stay in position even when there is a stretch involved. You'll want to land on your first finger on the 5th fret as you continue on to the third string.

Similarly, fingerings 1, 2, and 5 use fourth finger stretches: five out of six strings in fingering 1, two out of six in fingering 2, and four out of six in fingering 5. Fingering 4 uses a first finger stretch. Even though the first note played is F on the 1st fret, fingering 4 is actually in the 2nd fret position. Make sure your four fingers ultimately line up with frets 2, 3, 4, and 5, stretching only when you need to reach back for the F on the first fret of each E string.

Of course, you'll need to be able to play this in any key. No problem. Once you've learned all seven of these fingerings, you'll be able to transpose them easily. Here's a quick reference:

Sharp Keys						
1	**2**	**3**	**4**	**5**	**6**	**7**
C	D	E	F	G	A	B
G	A	B	C	D	E	F♯
D	E	F♯	G	A	B	C♯
A	B	C♯	D	E	F♯	G♯
E	F♯	G♯	A	B	C♯	D♯
B	C♯	D♯	E	F♯	G♯	A♯
F♯	G♯	A♯	B	C♯	D♯	E♯
C♯	D♯	E♯	F♯	G♯	A♯	B♯

Flat Keys						
1	**2**	**3**	**4**	**5**	**6**	**7**
C	D	E	F	G	A	B
F	G	A	B♭	C	D	E
B♭	C	D	E♭	F	G	A
E♭	F	G	A♭	B♭	C	D
A♭	B♭	C	D♭	E♭	F	G
D♭	E♭	F	G♭	A♭	B♭	C
G♭	A♭	B♭	C♭	D♭	E♭	F
C♭	D♭	E♭	F♭	G♭	A♭	B♭

FIG. 2.2. Sharp and Flat Keys

I've used C major as a reference for both the sharp keys and the flat keys. Keep the numbers (scale degrees) lined up to correspond with each note in the scale. Now when you want to play, for example, G major from the third degree, you can quickly see that the starting note is B. Set yourself up on the 7th fret position (on the note B on the 6th string), and follow fingering 3 as shown in figure 2.2. D from the seventh degree? C♯, start on the 9th fret and play fingering 7. F from the fourth degree? B♭, start on the 6th fret and play fingering 4, and so on.

Just as important as learning the fingerings is learning the *applications* of the scale. Your ears need to be involved right along with your fingers in order to naturally use these major scales in your playing. Let's go back to the key of C to try this out. Here are some common progressions in any key: I VI II V, I II III IV, I IV V IV, and VI IV. In the key of C, these are the following chords.

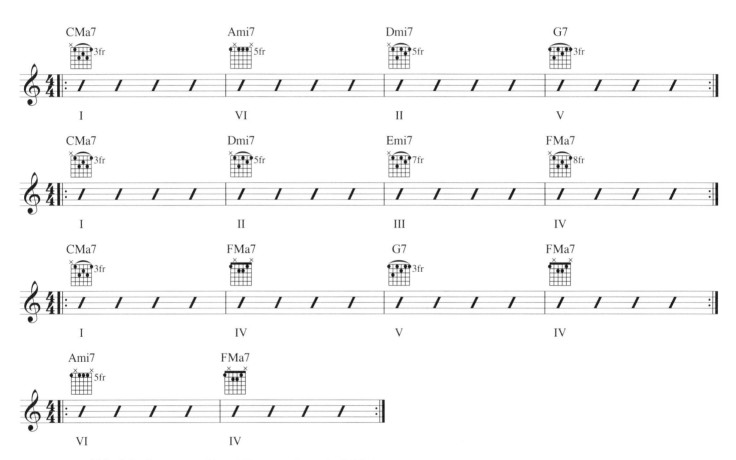

FIG. 2.3. Common Chord Progressions in C Major

Play these progressions as simply as you can. Record yourself; keep it simple here, too. A quick voice memo on your phone will do. Give yourself at least four repeats for each line, making the whole exercise long enough for you to work with, say ten or fifteen minutes total. As you listen to the playback, go ahead and practice those C major scale fingerings. You will no doubt hear the good match being made. Just playing the scale up and down will sound "right" with the diatonic chords in the same key. As your ears and fingers continue to work together, you might naturally begin to listen for phrases that you like as you play against the chords. Experiment with rhythms freely. You do not need to intellectualize this process now. Just listen as you practice.

CHAPTER 3

Scale Patterns

Once you have the seven major scale fingerings memorized, you can start using them to create melodies. You'll need some ideas beyond just playing the scale forward and backward, though. Patterns are an effective way to learn scales inside and out. In the process of learning patterns, you will be teaching your ears new melodies to reach for. Stopping, turning around, and starting in different places within a scale that you already know well can bring out fresh ideas and new angles in your melodies.

Patterns of *twos*, *threes*, and *fours* are ways to organize the notes in a scale so that you are playing in a jagged line rather than a straight line. Here is an example of twos played from scale fingering 7 in C major.

5   (0:00–0:36)

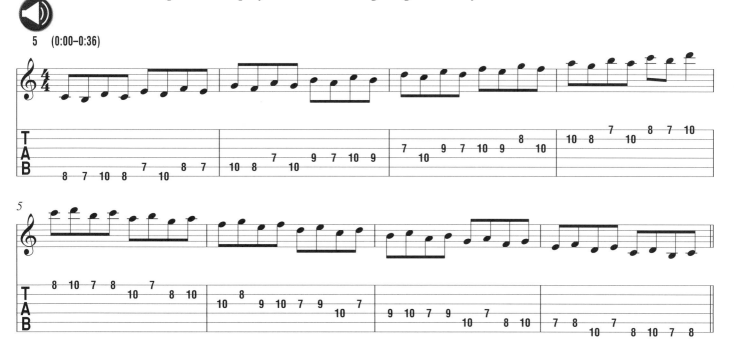

FIG. 3.1. Pattern of Twos with Scale Fingering 7 in C Major

You can think of this pattern as one step forward, one step backward as you ascend the scale. Turn it around to descend the scale without losing the flow of eighth notes. Next, play a pattern of *threes* as shown in figure 3.2, which you should naturally feel as eighth-note triplets.

FIG. 3.2. Pattern of Threes

Patterns of fours as sixteenth notes are shown in figure 3.3.

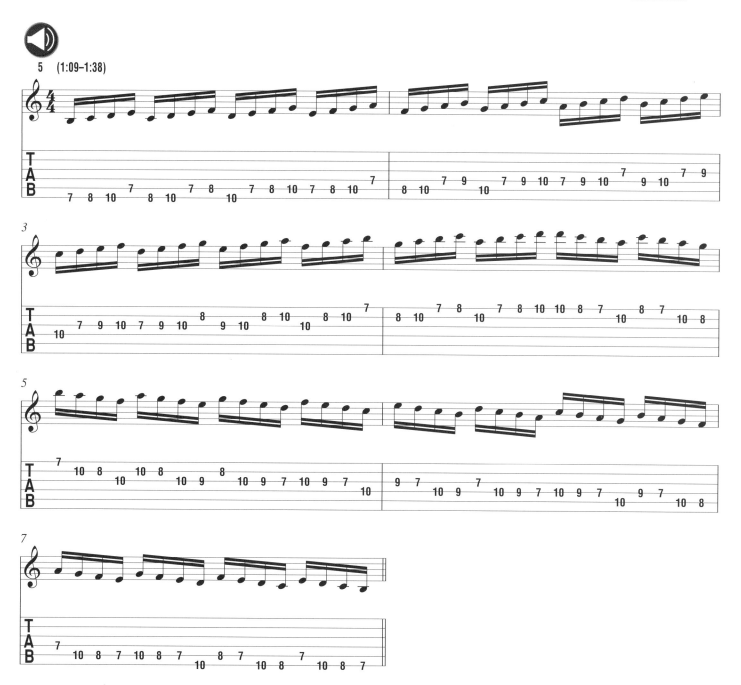

FIG. 3.3. Patterns of Fours

When practicing these patterns, use a metronome set at a very slow tempo to begin; 56 to 60 bpm tops. Start with the scale played forward and backward as quarter notes, then go right into the twos as eighth notes, threes as triplets, and fours as sixteenth notes without stopping between patterns. Once you can play the sixteenth notes comfortably at that tempo, gradually increase the metronome setting. You can set goals for yourself, such as to play sixteenth notes fluently at 72 bpm by Friday.

Practice twos, threes, and fours for all seven major scale fingerings, always starting at a slow tempo and gradually increasing your speed. Remember that the objective here is to create melodies by having your fingers teach your ears new patterns. Put this to work right away by playing over backing tracks. You can use the same tracks you made in chapter 2, or play any progression that you'd like that stays diatonic to C major.

Once you're well on your way to smoothing out the twists and turns of the twos, threes, and fours played all the way through each scale fingering, try repeating phrases and skipping around to different parts of the scale. The line below hangs on a phrase created from fours in the middle of the C major scale fingering 3.

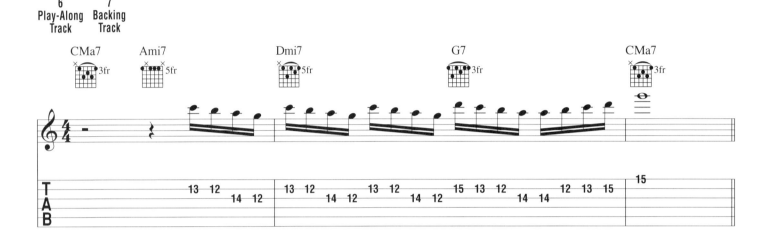

FIG. 3.4. Scale Fragment from Scale Fingering 3

Figure 3.5 shows some playfulness with the rhythm of fours. You've probably been feeling the fours quite naturally as sixteenth notes, since they are grouped in notes of four. Try feeling these groupings in a triplet rhythm, as shown.

8

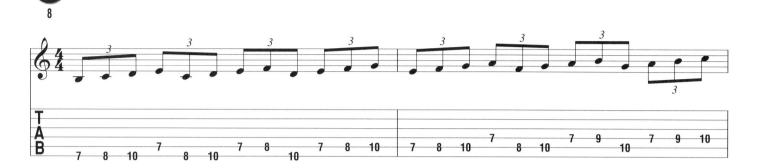

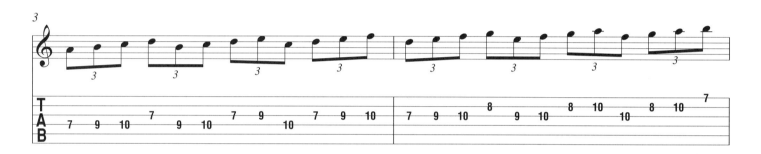

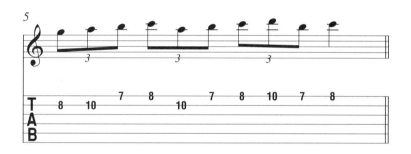

FIG. 3.5. Patterns of Fours in Triplets

Remember to keep practicing these lines with chords behind you. That will make it musical and a lot more fun.

CHAPTER 4

Backing Tracks

Practicing scales needs to be put into context. Hearing the relationship between scales and chords gets your ears involved in the process; it's what makes the practice of scales musical. You can find backing tracks (or "play-alongs") of all shapes and sizes almost everywhere you look. They are fun to use, and often provide an accurate time-keeping element. If you want to get better at *comping* (i.e., chordal accompaniment), however, create your own backing tracks so that you can comp for yourself. This is an opportunity for you to work on your accompaniment skills while you're working on creating melodies from scales.

You can keep the recording of yourself playing chords in time as simple as playing into your phone's voice memo capabilities, or you can go the more formal route and use more sophisticated recording software.

To start, create a backing track by playing a I VI II V in any key. Eventually, you'll hit all of the keys, but start with the one that corresponds to that new scale you've been memorizing. First, record it without a click track or metronome. Go around several times until you think you have enough. Play it back, and go ahead and solo along to your new track. Is it fun? Are you fighting at all with the comper in terms of time, feel, or busyness? Make some good honest observations about your comping from the perspective of the soloist. What do you need from that player? Start over, and try to give that to the next soloist (you, ten minutes later).

Record a new track, and this time, use a click. See chapter 6 for some metronome ideas. Create this new track based on what you learned from using the previous one. If you were too busy the last time, try to lay it down more simply this time. If you were too vague or not present enough last time, try to be clearer about your role as timekeeper and harmonic-describer this time. If you were jumping all over the neck playing a disjointed version of the chord progression, try keeping the chords closer together this time. Finally, make this pass extra long, because no matter how long the comping track feels while you're recording, it often just isn't long enough for the soloist (you).

Try another solo against this new backing track. Is the comper annoying you at all? Are you having to think too much about the time feeling weird, or are you able to just float on over it all and enjoy the experience? Do you want to hire that comper for a gig? Would you recommend that player? What feedback can you give that comper to help him or her improve?

Listen to commercial recordings, and focus on the comping that is going on. You will be ever more sensitive to comping that feels and sounds good to you, and that works in the overall context of the ensemble.

CHAPTER 5

Fill the Space

Sometimes, a little filler is called for in a song. You might be accompanying a singer, you might be accompanying yourself, you might be comping in a group setting. While it's perfectly all right to occasionally just keep a strum going during a break in the melodic action, there will be times when a scale fragment or short line is just the thing. Your first step is to let go of any attachments you might have to certain chord fingerings. The A triad shape on the 2nd fret is fine, but it takes up three out of four of your fretting fingers. One solution is to make a half-barre on the 2nd, 3rd, and 4th strings. You can either block the high E string, or use your fourth finger to play the high A on the 5th fret. Compare these two fingerings:

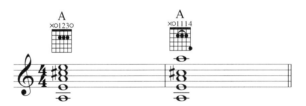

FIG. 5.1. Two Fingerings for A Major

You've freed up two fingers, which is considerable when it comes to scales and melodies. In fact, you've allowed your fourth finger to reach the high A, which would not have been possible using the three finger A, so you've effectively opened up three more fingers to use. Here's a line you can reach without letting go of that chord.

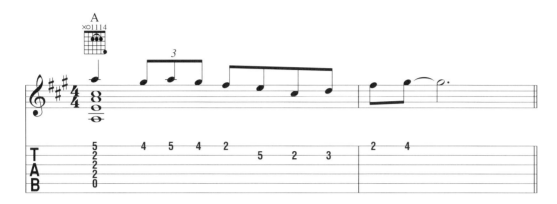

FIG. 5.2. A Chord with Melody

You'll hear this line naturally in the key of A. What if the A chord is actually functioning as the V chord in the key of D? Try this:

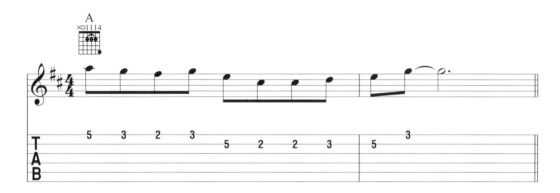

FIG. 5.3. A Chord with Melody in D

Free up some fingers of a D chord by making a half barre on the first three strings and adding your second finger to the D note instead of tying up three fingers.

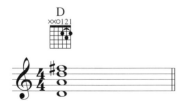

FIG. 5.4. D Chord with Half Barre

Play this melody while holding down as much of the chord as you can. You can either lean your second finger across the first two strings to play the G natural, or simply let go of the 2nd string.

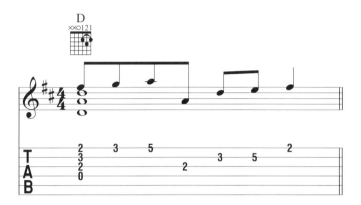

FIG. 5.5. D Chord with Melody

The G natural sounds right, right? Listen to the G♯ in the melody here:

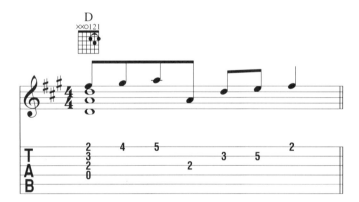

FIG 5.6. D Chord with Melody in A

The G♯ might sound like a wrong note until you hear it in the context of the key of A, like this:

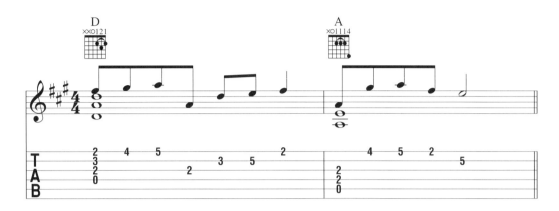

FIG. 5.7. Melody with Chords in A

Even just a bass note can be effective to hold down while fingering a line from a scale on top of it. The first measure below suggests a G chord without having to play the whole chord at once.

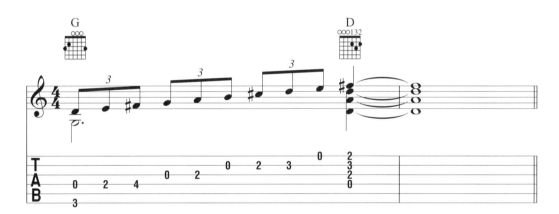

FIG. 5.8. D Scale with G and D in Bass

CHAPTER 6

Metronome Tips

Time really is of the essence when it comes to playing jazz. Guitarists can play two roles in a jazz band: melody player/soloist, and part of the rhythm section, comping. Playing melodies—improvised lines in particular—requires thinking of rhythms apart from the rhythm that anyone else is playing while still playing in time and with feeling appropriate for the overall groove. The exercises in this chapter will bring your playing to life by getting you to make conscious choices about the rhythms you play, rather than losing sight of the rhythm of the melodic lines in favor of just finding the "right" notes.

15
"Leaves"
Demo
Track

16
"Leaves"
Backing
Track

Begin with a song that you know well. It could be a jazz standard, it could be a general chord progression, or an original piece of music. It can be in any time signature. Set a metronome click at a fairly slow tempo, say 60 bpm. Record yourself playing the chords for four choruses. On playback, improvise in the following manner: play all eighth notes for the first chorus, all eighth note triplets for the second chorus, and all sixteenth notes for the third chorus. For the fourth and last chorus, allow yourself to play anything you want. Any note, any rhythm.

Typically, you'll leave a lot of space in that last chorus! It will be a relief not to have to play anything steadily through with no interruption, especially those sixteenth notes. More importantly, by then, you'll be tuned in to what rhythm you are playing at any given point in the solo. When you are free to make the choice, you will become very effective in the use of rhythms to make a melodic statement.

If your ideas dry up during any of the steady choruses, just stay on one note while making the time and the rhythm of that chorus the top priority. You'll be surprised how effective that can be in structuring an improvised line. If you've never considered the rhythm of a melody very much as you play, the metronome will point out ways in which your time has been inconsistent. It will feel great when each consecutive chorus lines up with the clicks.

17
"Rain"
Demo
Track

18
"Rain"
Backing
Track

You've probably counted time in eighth notes before, whether or not you were aware of doing it: "1 and 2 and 3 and 4 and." When it comes to triplets, say "1 trip-let 2 trip-let," etc., or you can say "trip-a-let trip-a-let" or any three syllable word that will help you to feel it. For sixteenth notes, use "1-ee-and-a 2-ee-and-a," or you can say the word "wa-ter-mel-on wa-ter-mel-on" or any four-syllable word that will help you feel it as you play. Next, increase the tempo and repeat the four choruses. You can move the metronome setting to 72, for example, but another way to use the metronome for time keeping is to cut the tempo in half. Now the metronome will be indicating half notes instead of quarter notes. Setting the metronome at 36 will put the real tempo at 72. If you want to play straight eighth notes, as in a Latin or rock feel, count the clicks as 1, 3, 1, 3, etc. Repeat the four choruses and notice what that does for your time keeping as you comp and as you improvise.

19
"Leaves"
Demo
Track

20
"Leaves"
Backing
Track

If you want to swing those eighth notes, then it is best to count the clicks as 2, 4, 2, 4, etc. They will still be half notes, but you will be supplying your own beats 1 and 3 in your head. The swing feel will be inevitable. You will feel the clicks the same as if you were playing with a very reliable drummer stressing 2 and 4 on the hi-hat. Repeat the four choruses this way. Remember to go through the entire series of eighth, triplet, and sixteenth notes as you play along before you get to the "anything you want" part. You can decide if the metronome will be clicking on every beat, or as half notes.

21

In 3/4 time, you can set the metronome on every click the way you would to indicate quarter notes.

22

You could also give it a jazz waltz feel by hearing two clicks per measure of 3, resulting in two dotted quarter notes. If you want the tempo to be 100, set the metronome at 50.

23

For an extra challenge in 3/4, try making the click play on beat 1 only of every measure. If you want to play at 120, set the metronome at 40 and fill in your own beats 2 and 3 in your mind's ear.

Spend an hour or so going through your chosen song several times, changing the tempo after every completed cycle of soloing with your awareness on the rhythms you choose. Make random leaps in the tempo each time you begin a new cycle. Start at 60, next time use 112, next time take it back to 72 using two clicks per bar. Mix it up.

CHAPTER 7

Seventh Chords

To find whatever it is you're looking for on the guitar, start with something you know, and then manipulate it or alter it to transform that into something that you need. For example, look at a D triad.

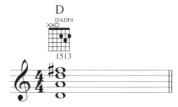

FIG. 7.1. D Major Triad

Name the notes across the neck from the D bass note: D A D F♯. Now, identify how those notes function in the chord: 1 5 1 3. You know from studying theory that to turn a major chord into a minor chord, flat the 3. That means if you lower the F♯ by one fret to turn it into F, you'll be playing a D minor triad.

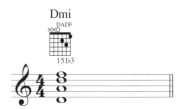

FIG. 7.2. D Minor Triad

That's an easy one to see. Here are two more to get you primed for more adventurous ones to follow:

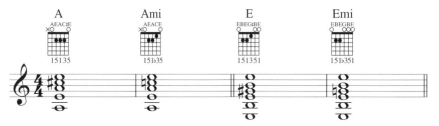

FIG. 7.3. A Major and Minor and E Major and Minor

Any of these A chords can be moved up the neck under a barre, so once you know Ami7, you can easily find Bmi7 here:

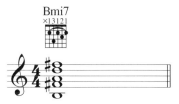

FIG. 7.10. Bmi7 Barre Chord

E chords work under a barre as well. EMa7, E7, Emi7:

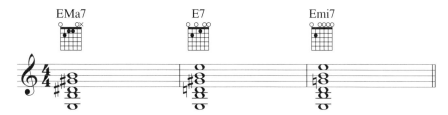

FIG. 7.11. E Chord Forms for Barre Chords

Often, a better choice for a major 7 chord with the root on the 6th string is this:

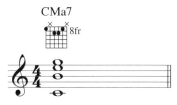

FIG. 7.12. CMa7, no Barre

It saves you from having to make a barre, and it sounds cleaner.

Here are two ways to play seventh chords in any key diatonically ascending from the root:

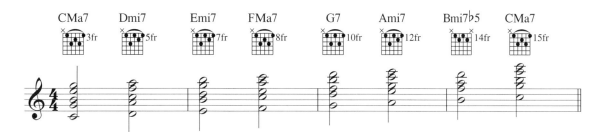

FIG. 7.13. Diatonic Chords from Root 5

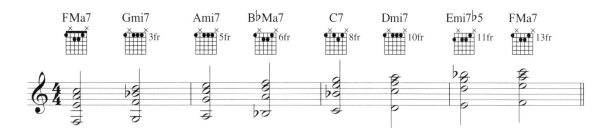

FIG. 7.14. Diatonic Chords from Root 6

CHAPTER 8

Tensions and Extensions

Adding interest to chords is a hallmark of jazz comping. The chords go beyond the basic triads and often beyond seventh chords, too. If you can create seventh chords, then you can create chords with tensions or extensions. The basic premise is to build the chord by going through the scale in thirds. For example, a CMa9 is 1 3 5 7 9, or C E G B D in the C major scale. To alter a tension, change the note that is naturally occurring in the scale. For example, C7(♭9) is 1 3 5 ♭7 ♭9 or C E G B♭ D♭. Just as you found seventh chords from triads you already knew (see chapter 7), you can find natural and altered tensions starting with seventh chords that you know. Keep this shortcut in mind when it comes to naming tensions: 9 is the same note name as 2, 11 is the same note name as 4, and 13 is the same note name as 6. Here is a list of chord formulas to get started:

Chord Type	Formula	Chord Symbol
Major 9	1 3 5 7 9	CMa9
Major 9 (♯11)	1 3 5 7 9 ♯11	CMa9(♯11)
6(9)	1 3 5 6 9	C6(9)
Add 9	1 3 5 9	Cadd9 or C(9)
Dominant 9	1 3 5 ♭7 9	C7(9) or C9
Dominant 7 (♭9)	1 3 5 ♭7 ♭9	C7(♭9)
Dominant 7 (♯9)	1 3 5 ♭7 ♯9	C7(♯9)
Dominant 7 (13)	1 3 5 ♭7 13	C7(13)
Dominant 7 (♭13)	1 3 5 ♭7 ♭13	C7(♭13)
Minor 9	1 ♭3 5 ♭7 9	Cmi9 or C–9 or Cmin9
Minor 7 (11)	1 ♭3 5 ♭7 11	Cmi7(11) or C–7(11) or C–11
Minor add 9	1 ♭3 5 9	Cmi(add9) or Cmin(add9) or C–(9)

FIG. 8.1. Chords with Tensions

CHAPTER 9

Chord Voicings and Spellings

Questions: Quick, what's the 13 on a B♭7 chord? What's the ♭9 of F7? The ♯5 of E♭7? The ♯11 on DMa9?

Chord symbols are a wonderful shorthand to the language of music. They spell out the chord as succinctly as possible. Dmi7♭5 is just a brilliant use of language; it's clear and to the point.

If you have an understanding of theory and chord construction, you will quickly see how you can identify and memorize notes all over the neck. This helps your sight-reading, helps your improvising, gets you playing in positions on the neck different from your usual places, and it helps you to think quickly while you're playing.

Answers: the 13 on a B♭7 is . . . G! The ♭9 of F7: G♭. The ♯5 of E♭7: B. The ♯11 on DMa9: G♯ (valuable shortcut to note names of tensions: 9 = 2, 11 = 4, 13 = 6, as related to the root of the chord and the major scale of the same name).

Take a closer look at these chords to find some voicing options. The first B♭7 shown is a nice three-note voicing containing the root, ♭7, and 3, or B♭, A♭, and D in this case.

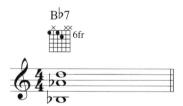

FIG. 9.1. B♭7 in a Three-Note Voicing

There's a G handily within reach on the second string 8th fret. Your fourth finger can grab that. Now you have a B♭7(13).

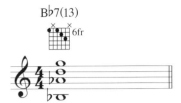

FIG. 9.2. Adding 13 to B♭7

Note that you're easily blocking the fifth string with your first finger, and blocking the first string with your fourth finger. Being accurate with your picking style or finger style approach with your picking hand will provide the needed blocks as well.

Move the whole works down one fret, or a half step, to A7(13).

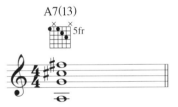

FIG. 9.3. Movable Chord Form Down a Half Step

The note names have changed, but the associated numbers—i.e., 1, ♭7, 3, and 13—remain the same. Quick, what's the 13 on an A7 chord? . . . F♯. Therefore, that's an F♯ that your fourth finger is now playing.

Move it up to the 8th fret so C is the root. What's the 13 of a C7? A. Your fourth finger on the 10th fret is playing the note A. Of course, don't leave out the others. What's the 3 of a C7? E. Your third finger has that one covered. Soon, you'll never forget that E is the 9th fret on the G string. What's the ♭7 of C7? B♭. Your second finger is covering that one for us, D string 8th fret.

Another handy three-note voicing for a dominant 7 chord is shown with the root on the 5th string.

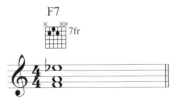

FIG. 9.4. F7 with Root on 5th String

The F7 on the 8th fret gives us F, A, and E♭, or root, 3, and ♭7. To that, you can add a number of nearby tensions. The example on the next page shows the ♭9, which we've identified as G♭.

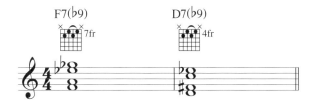

FIG. 9.5. Adding ♭9 to a Dominant Chord

Move it to D7(♭9) by bringing it all down to the root on the 5th fret. What is the ♭9 on a D7 chord, according to your theory study? E♭. Your first finger on the 2nd string, then, is playing E♭.

E♭7♯5 (also called E♭+7, or E♭aug7) can be fingered as shown.

FIG. 9.6. Augmented Fingering Option

We've already seen that the first three fingers are making a dominant 7 chord form. The 12th fret on the B string is B, or the ♯5 of E♭. Your fourth finger has now identified that chord tone, which can similarly be moved around the neck to show any ♯5.

Notation Note: It's common to abbreviate chord symbols by leaving out the 7 sometimes and just saying the tensions. DMa7(9) and DMa9 actually indicate the same chord.

So, here, DMa9 is shown at the 5th fret.

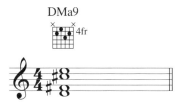

FIG. 9.7. DMa9 on 5th Fret

Make a barre with your first finger to catch the G♯(♯11) on the 4th fret of the E string. What's the ♯11 of GMa7(9,♯11)? C♯. Move the ♯11 chord form to the 10th fret to play the root on G, and you'll find the C♯ on the 9th fret of the E string.

Make a habit of identifying all of the notes in every chord you play or learn. Then identify how those notes function in the chord. Remember that the note names will change as the chord moves, but the numbers will not change. The next time you are reading music, you will be pleased to see how quickly you can find that F♯ on the 7th fret of the B string.

CHAPTER 10

II V I Progressions

The progression of IImi7 V7 IMa7 is so common in jazz that it is very important to memorize it, know it when you see it, and know several different ways to play the chords in any key. No doubt you've played II V's before, if you've played any popular music at all. Ami D is an example of a II V in G.

First, review where the chords come from. In the key of C, the second chord—or the II chord—is Dmi7. The V chord is G7. For now, assume that the II V will resolve to I, although that won't always be the case in all songs. The I chord will match the name of the key, so in this case, it is CMa7. Listen to the sound of the chords, record yourself playing them, and pay extra attention to the sound of the root motion—meaning the bass notes—with D going to G going to C.

26

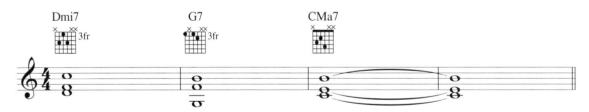

FIG. 10.1. II V I in C

Complete this worksheet to help you to memorize all of the II V I progressions in each key. The answers are upside down.

IImi7	V7	IMa7
Dmi7	G7	CMa7
	D7	GMa7
Emi7		DMa7
Bmi7	E7	
F#mi7		
	F#7	BMa7
G#mi7	C#7	
	G#7	
Gmi7	C7	
	F7	B♭Ma7
	B♭7	
B♭mi7	E♭7	
E♭mi7	A♭7	
	D♭7	G♭Ma7
	G♭7	

Answers:

IImi7	V7	IMa7
Dmi7	G7	CMa7
Ami7	D7	GMa7
Emi7	A7	DMa7
Bmi7	E7	AMa7
F#mi7	B7	EMa7
C#mi7	F#7	BMa7
G#mi7	C#7	F#Ma7
D#mi7	G#7	C#Ma7
Gmi7	C7	FMa7
Cmi7	F7	B♭Ma7
Fmi7	B♭7	E♭Ma7
B♭mi7	E♭7	A♭Ma7
E♭mi7	A♭7	D♭Ma7
A♭mi7	D♭7	G♭Ma7
D♭mi7	G♭7	C♭Ma7

FIG. 10.2. II V I Worksheet

If you already know how to play barre chord versions of these chords, you will see how easily you can move them around the neck to play in all keys. Dmi7 G7 CMa7 could be played beginning with a root 5 version of Dmi7 going to a root 6 version of G7 resolving to a root 5 version of CMa7. Or you could play it beginning with Dmi7 as a root 6 barre chord. But don't stop there. Let go of the barre and add some tensions, like these:

27

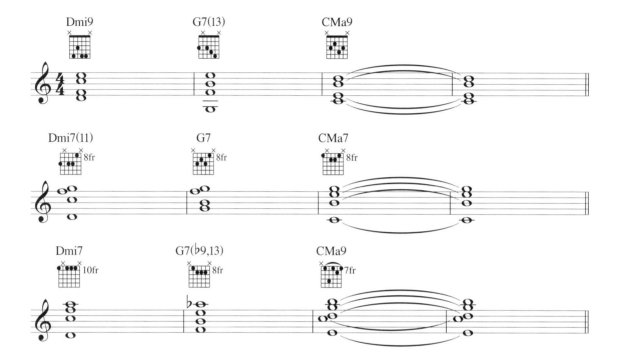

FIG. **10.3.** II V I Voicings with Tensions in C

Practice these chord forms in every key.

CHAPTER 11

A II V I Lick

To learn any language, idioms or phrases are useful to hold your own in conversation. If you say, "Hi, how's it going?" you're not likely to encounter any harsh criticism for un-originality. ("Oh, how derivative. I just said that to someone earlier today....") It is simply an icebreaker; a place to start a conversation. Similarly, in jazz improvisation, you'll need some places to start when it's your turn to speak.

Here is a typical boppish line to learn and analyze. It is played over a II V I progression. I like to tell my students that it is a good one to memorize in case you ever see any II Vs.

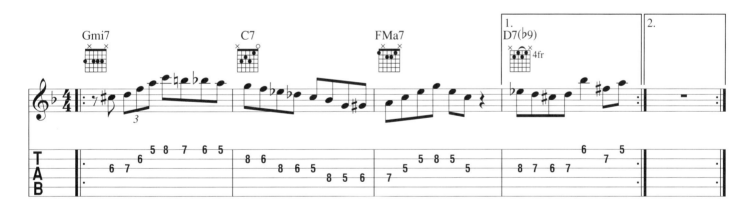

FIG. 11.1. A Lick over a II V I

Learn this in all keys by working out a fingering in 5th position for the key of F. Try it on your own, first. Then, refer to the fingerings in figure 11.2 to compare notes.

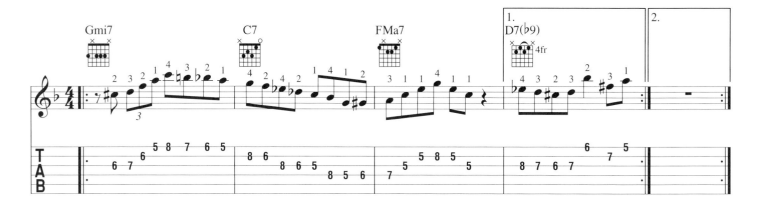

FIG. 11.2. Fingerings for the II V I Lick

Listen to the melody against the chords to get a deep understanding of what the line is saying. Improvising is very much like speaking off the cuff, which is easy enough to do when you know your topic well. Knowing the chord progression is like knowing your topic.

Look at the Dmi triad contained in the melody of measure 1. The chord at that point is Gmi7. A Dmi triad creates a nice Gmi9 there. In measure 2, tension abounds with the notes E♭ to D♭ against the C7 chord. Enharmonically, E♭ is D♯, or the ♯9 of the chord, while D♭ is the ♭9. The measure ends with a G♯, which is enharmonically A♭, or ♭13 of the C7. Once that resolves to the F chord, the melody line makes an Ami7 arpeggio, which is the upper structure, or the top notes, of an FMa9. The *turnaround*—the chords that pull the whole thing musically back to the top before a repeat—provides plenty of tension against the D7 chord, which will surely come in handy in the future any time you want to alter a dominant chord. E♭ is the ♭9, B♭ is the ♭13. The jagged line between the B♭ and the F♯ to the A is an effective way to bring it back to the top, or Gmi7.

Once you are comfortable with the melody, you'll need to play it in every key.

28
Play-Along Track

29
Backing Track

To practice this, use the play-along track provided, or make your own. I suggest going around the cycle in fourths. Doing this is a great way to hit every key without simply moving up or down chromatically. Playing in fourths will provide a natural resolution from one key to the next.

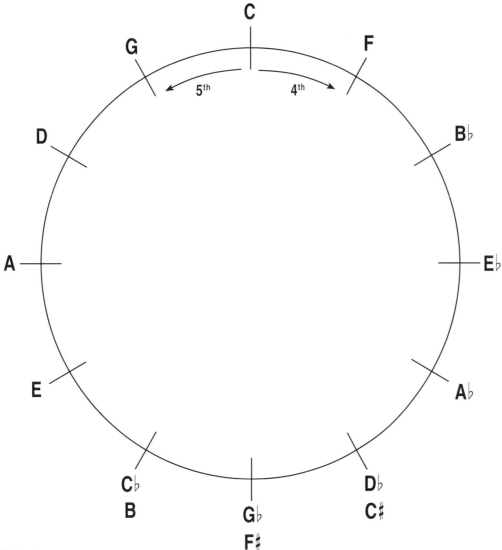

FIG. 11.3. Circle of Fourths

Transpose the chords in figure 11.1 to play each key in the same way, including the repeat. This will be excellent practice for memorizing II V I's, if you haven't yet (see chapter 10). You can use the Circle of Fourths chart to help you find the chords. II V I progressions use three adjacent roots in a row moving clockwise.

On playback, set up in the corresponding position to play the line in the right key as follows:

The line in the key of F is played in 5th position. Think "A," which is the note your first finger is covering on the low E string. "A" is 3 of F. "A" is also the 9 of the IImi7 chord (Gmi7)

To change keys, ask: what is the 3 of the new key? Set up so that your first finger is on that note on the low E string and play the fingering that you have worked out for the above line. Or ask, what is 9 of the new key's IImi7 chord, set up in that position, and play the line. Either approach will put you in the same place.

For example: new key of B♭; 3 of the key is D. Set up on the 10th fret position, play the line. The 9 of the IImi7 chord (Cmi7) is D. Again, set up in 10th fret position.

You will hear when it is right as you play along to a backing track.

CHAPTER 12

Guide Tones

All seventh chords contain guide tones: they are the 3 and the 7 of the chord. The most important information about the quality of the chord is contained in these two notes. The 3 of the chord tells you if it is major or minor. The 7 tells you if it is major or dominant or minor. Your ears will adjust to the sound of a chord if the root is not being played. The guide tones are really all you need. Here is a G7 resolving to CMa7:

FIG. 12.1. G7 to CMa7

The 3 of G7 is B and the 7 is F. The guide tones of CMa7 are E and B. There is only a one note—in fact, a half-step—difference between the guide tones of those two chords. Listen to the resolution from just those notes.

30

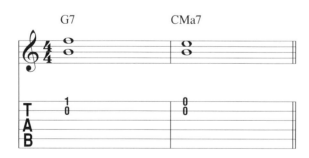

FIG. 12.2. Guide Tone Resolution G7 to C

Add the root to your fingering if you wish, but after a few times, you won't even need the root to hear how powerful those guide tones are on their own.

Just as all seventh chords have guide tones, all seventh chord progressions have guide-tone lines. Pick one of the two possible guide tones of the first chord. From there, continue to the nearest guide tone of the next chord. Do that all the way through the chord progression. It is a perfect line to thread through the chords, since each guide tone states the essence of the chord. Moving the shortest distance from one guide tone to the next makes the smoothest possible line.

Here's a guide-tone line to study, play, and hear.

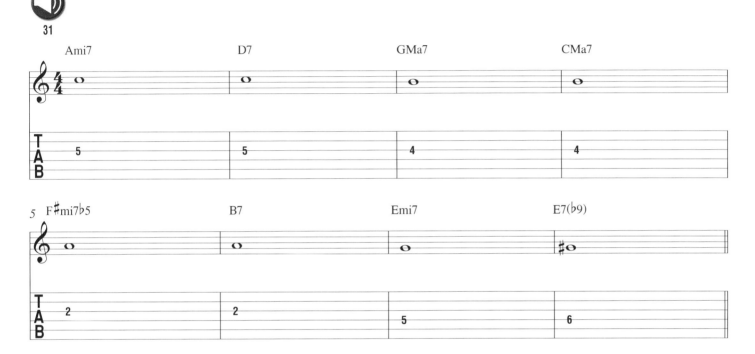

FIG. 12.3. Guide-Tone Line Study

If you start on the other choice of a guide tone from the beginning, everything that follows will change. Here, then, is the second possible guide-tone
line in the same progression.

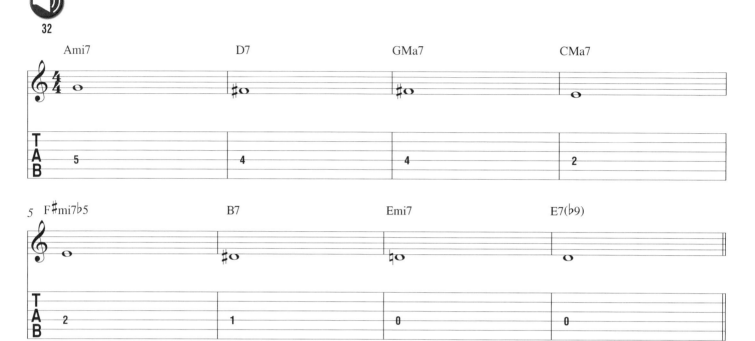

FIG. 12.4. Guide-Tone Line

Notice how the guide-tone line follows the same harmonic rhythm as the
chords themselves. These lines are often used as background lines for horn
parts or "oohs" and "ahhs" for singers. They also make for good starting places
in an improvised line over the chords. Just adding a few embellishments to the
guide-tone lines will demonstrate possibilities for taking a solo that captures
the essence of each chord.

33 Play-Along Track 34 Backing Track

FIG. 12.5. Embellished Guide-Tone Line

Whenever you listen to music, take some time to identify the guide-tone lines in your mind's ear. It's a good way to practice your ear training without having your guitar in your hands.

CHAPTER 13

Dominant Substitutions

You can hear the resolution of G7 to C (V7 to I) coming a mile away. The guide tones tell the story and the root motion provides the structure. We know that the guide tones of a G7 chord are B (3) and F (♭7). Move the F to E, and you'll be left with the guide tones of the CMa7 chord where it has resolved. Jazz players (and composers and arrangers) use dominant substitution to change things up a bit without sacrificing the way the original chord is functioning. On close examination, you'll see that only the root motion changes when playing a dominant substitution.

The shortcut for finding the appropriate substitution for a dominant chord is to think up one-half step from the root of the target chord (in our example, C is the target). So D♭7 replaces G7. Compare the two, shown below:

FIG. 13.1. Dominant Substitution in C

We've identified the guide tones of the G7 already: B and F. Now, name the guide tones of the D♭7 chord. The 3 is F and the ♭7 is C♭. C♭ is also known as B, enharmonically, so these two chords contain the same guide tones! They are inverted; B and F in G7 and F and B in D♭7. Play and listen to the guide tones below, both resolving to C. Don't play the bass notes yet.

35

FIG. 13.2. Dominant Substitution Guide Tones

Now, add the bass notes. It is only then that you hear the difference between the two dominant chords.

Dominant substitution is also called "tritone" substitution. For one thing, the roots of the two dominant chords are the interval of a tritone apart. More importantly, the two chords contain the same guide tones, and guide tones in a dominant seventh chord are always a tritone apart (B and F, F and B).

DOMINANT SUBSTITUTE PRACTICE

Here is a worksheet to fill in the missing chords. The progressions on the left are the original diatonic chords; the progressions on the right have dominant substitutions. Take a minute to write in the missing chords, and then play through each progression to make sure your ears are completely involved in the process.

36

Diatonic				Dominant Substitutes		
IImi7	V7	I		IImi7	♭II7	I
Dmi7	G7	CMa7		Dmi7	D♭7	CMa7
Gmi7		FMa7		Gmi7	G♭7	
	F7			Cmi7		B♭Ma7
Fmi7		E♭Ma7		Fmi7		
	E♭7	A♭Ma7				A♭Ma7
E♭mi7		D♭Ma7			D7	D♭Ma7
	D♭7	G♭Ma7		A♭mi7	G7	
	F♯7	BMa7		C♯mi7		BMa7
F♯mi7		EMa7		F♯mi7		EMa7
Bmi7	E7			Bmi7		AMa7
		DMa7			E♭7	
Ami7		GMa7		Ami7		GMa7

FIG. 13.3. Dominant Substitutes Practice

Diatonic			Dominant Substitutes		
IImi7	V7	I	IImi7	♭II7	I
Dmi7	G7	CMa7	Dmi7	D♭7	CMa7
Gmi7	C7	FMa7	Gmi7	G♭7	FMa7
Cmi7	F7	B♭Ma7	Cmi7	B7	B♭Ma7
Fmi7	B♭7	E♭Ma7	Fmi7	E7	E♭Ma7
B♭mi7	E♭7	A♭Ma7	B♭mi7	A7	A♭Ma7
E♭mi7	A♭7	D♭Ma7	E♭mi7	D7	D♭Ma7
A♭mi7	D♭7	G♭Ma7	A♭mi7	G7	G♭Ma7
C♯mi7	F♯7	BMa7	C♯mi7	C7	BMa7
F♯mi7	B7	EMa7	F♯mi7	F7	EMa7
Bmi7	E7	AMa7	Bmi7	B♭7	AMa7
Emi7	A7	DMa7	Emi7	E♭7	DMa7
Ami7	D7	GMa7	Ami7	A♭7	GMa7

FIG. 13.4. Dominant Substitutes Practice (Answers)

CHAPTER 14

The Melodic Minor Scale

The melodic minor scale has evolved from its early traditional days of being identified as a natural minor scale with a raised 6 and 7 as it is ascending, and reverting back to a natural minor scale as it is descending. Popular music, and jazz in particular, now most commonly uses the melodic minor scale the same way whether it is going up or down. It is easiest to think of the melodic minor as a major scale with a flat third. Consider the A natural minor scale:

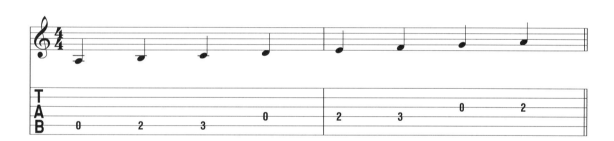

FIG. 14.1. A Natural Minor

By definition, the melodic minor scale has a raised 6 and 7 as compared to natural minor, so here is A melodic minor:

FIG. 14.2. A Melodic Minor

Now, look at an A major scale:

FIG. 14.3. A Major

The only difference between A major and A melodic minor is the C♯ and C natural, respectively.

To work out fingerings for this versatile and essential scale in jazz playing, go back to your major scale fingering (see chapter 2) and flat the thirds in all of them. It is especially important to tune into Do while playing through these scales both as major and as melodic minor. If you know where Do is, you will easily be able to find—and hear—Mi, or the third degree of the scale. Playing the ♭3 to make the scale minor will become natural, and you won't have to think about it consciously after a little practice.

Here are seven fingerings for C melodic minor. Before memorizing these fingerings, use the seven different C major scale fingerings that you now know, and flat the 3's, as described above. Then look on the following page and compare notes with yourself as to what fingerings work well.

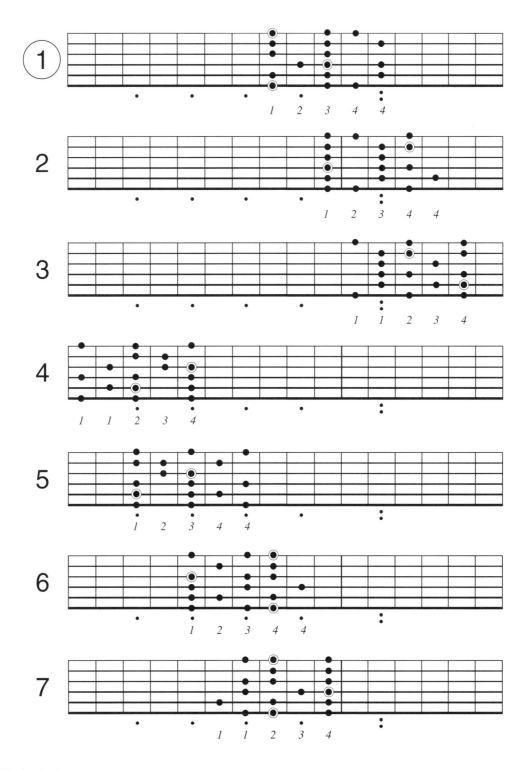

FIG. 14.4. C Melodic Minor Fingerings

Just as you transposed the C major scales to every key in chapter 2, learn these fingerings in every key as well.

Melodic Minor Scale Applications

The melodic minor scale brings new and exciting information for your ears if you've used mostly major or pentatonic scales in your playing until now. For starters, look at how many whole steps fall consecutively in this scale:

FIG. 15.1. Whole Steps of C Melodic Minor Scale

E♭ F G A B: all whole steps. That is a wide-open sound for your mind's ear to learn and begin to call for in your improvising. Here, now, are three applications for the scale.

First, play a Cmi chord. Make it Cmi7 if you'd like. Make it Cmi6 if you'd like. A triad works just fine, too. The C melodic minor scale will sound cool against any of these chords, although the rub will be the B natural playing against the B♭ in the Cmi7 chord. The I chord in the melodic minor scale is Imi(Ma7). In our example, that is Cmi(Ma7), spelled C E♭ G B. Play that chord, then listen to the scale, and you will have a more obvious match. Here are some fingerings:

39

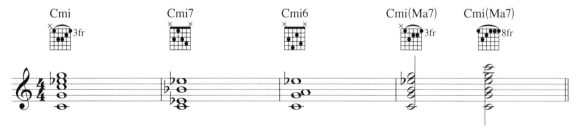

FIG. 15.2. Fingerings for C Minor Chords

Next, consider dominant seventh chords. Typically, they are thought of as V7, since the V chord in any major key is diatonically a dominant seventh chord. If that V7 chord is resolving to its I chord, as in G7 to C, then you can give that G7 some altered tensions to make the pull to C even stronger than if you just play G7. Play and listen to these examples:

40

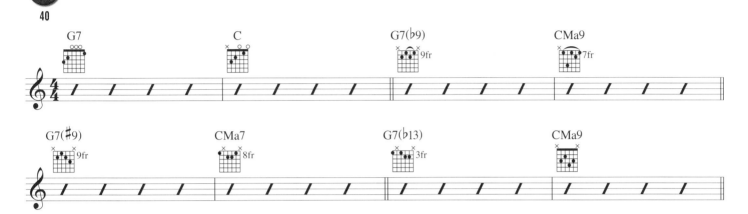

FIG. 15.3. Dominant Chords with Altered Tensions Resolving to I

That is a good rule of thumb for comping in jazz: alter the V7 chord if it is resolving to its I, whether the I is major or minor.

It follows that you'll want to bring out the altered sound of that dominant chord (which is just screaming to resolve) as you improvise lines over that chord.

Take a look at the A♭ melodic minor scale:

FIG. 15.4. A♭ Melodic Minor

If you relate each note in the scale to the G7 chord, you will see all of the altered tensions that we could choose to add to the chord. Even if the person comping doesn't add any tensions, you as improviser can!

The notes stack up this way against the G7: A♭ = ♭9, B♭ = ♯9, C♭ = 3, D♭ = ♭5, E♭ = ♭13, F = ♭7, G = 1, A♭ = ♭9. Practice with the backing track provided or make your own, in which you play G7 for two bars followed by CMa7 for two bars. Repeat the four bars several times. On playback, play the A♭ melodic minor scale during the G7, and switch to the C major scale during the CMa7. Here it is going up one way and down the other:

41
Play-Along
Track

42
Backing
Track

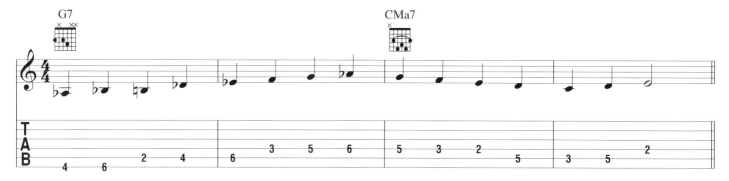

FIG. 15.5. A♭ Melodic Minor Resolving to C Major

Though this is just the two scales without any creative ideas thrown in yet, it sounds rich and full of tension and resolution. Your ears will embrace this sound as you practice, and it will begin to work itself into your playing. You will probably start hearing it as you listen to other players now. Your ears will be tuned in and you will recognize it as that sound you were getting in the practice room. This is good; you'll want to notice how players work with phrases and melodies from this scale beyond playing it from beginning to end.

There will be dominant chords that do not resolve, too. Figure 15.6 is an F7 that goes up one-half step and back, and then down one-half step and back. You won't want to alter any tensions you might add to these dominant chords, since you don't want to imply that they will resolve to their I chord and then disappoint the listener. Instead, play natural tensions on the dominant chords:

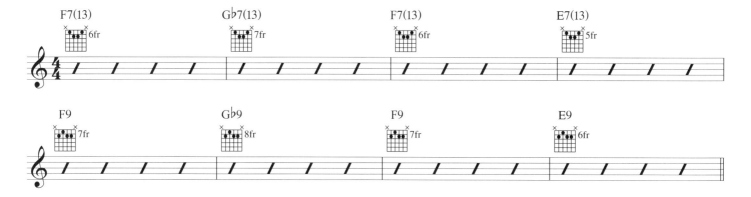

FIG. 15.6. Non-Resolving Dominant Chords with Natural Tensions

To play lines over the dominant chords that don't resolve, you will find the natural tensions—or extensions—in the melodic minor scale that is built from the 5th of the chord. So, play C melodic minor over F7(13). Analyze the notes related to the chord this time, and you'll see all of the good bright sounding natural tensions that go with the chord:

FIG. 15.7. C Melodic Minor Scale. C = 5, D = 13, E♭ = ♭7, F = 1, G = 9, A = 3, B = ♯11, C = 5

43
Demo
Track

44
Backing
Track

Play and record the chord progression for yourself. On playback, play and listen to C melodic minor, D♭ melodic minor, and B melodic minor, against each of the dominant chords. Here is a sample of those scales and chords together:

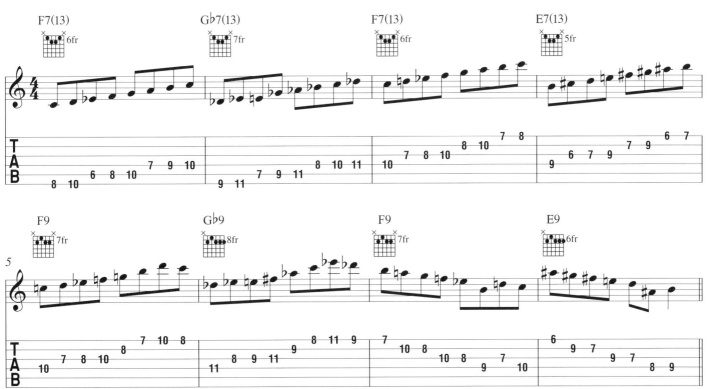

FIG. 15.8. Melodic Minor Scale Lines with Non-Resolving Dominant Chords

The big ear opener this time will be that big bright ♯11 sound that the scale brings. You'll start hearing that everywhere now, too!

It is a common dilemma for jazz players to be able to fit the scale that they want to hear into a short space. Sometimes, you'll only have two beats to make some sort of statement about that dominant 7 chord. This makes the case for learning patterns, which will get you playing the scale from every point along the way, stopping and starting on different notes. Another way to free yourself from the self-imposed constraint of playing the scale from beginning to end is to pare down a bit and play arpeggios. As mentioned, the I chord in any melodic minor scale is Imi(Ma7). Against that G7(♭13) chord, look what an A♭mi(Ma7) will give you: A♭ = ♭9, C♭ (B) = 3, E♭ = ♭13, G = 1. If you add a 9 to the A♭mi(Ma7) arpeggio, you will be adding B♭, or the ♯9 of G7. Here are two fingerings for the A♭mi9(Ma7):

45

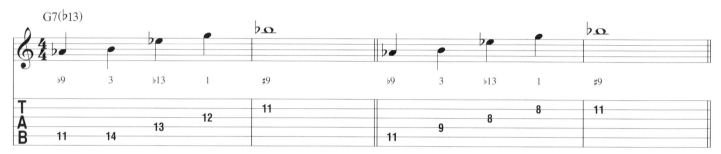

FIG. 15.9. Two Ways to Play A♭mi(Ma7)

The arpeggios give you all of the rich tensions found in the scale, condensed to a shorter phrase to play. Make it resolve to CMa7 by arpeggiating that chord, just to hear things pared down there, too.

Here is a progression to practice, along with an idea for lines taken from the corresponding melodic minor scales. Create your own lines this way using these chords, and also transpose to other keys.

46
Demo
Track

47
Backing
Track

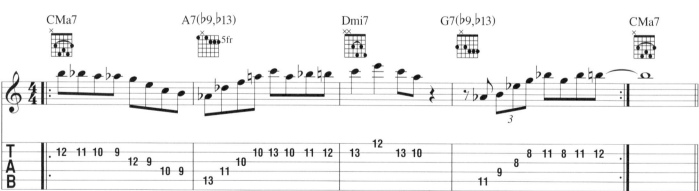

FIG. 15.10. Sample Line Using Melodic Minor Scale Applications

CHAPTER 16

Drop-2 Voicings

It is essential to have a large collection of chord forms at your disposal in order to be fluent in comping. Comping chords effectively and naturally requires an ease of changing and recognizing positions for chords wherever you happen to be on the neck. If you know only one or two ways to play each chord, then you've likely encountered a problem when you have to shift dramatically from one chord to another, disrupting the flow of the music and potentially losing your place on the neck. I like to think of chord forms as Starbucks. You shouldn't have too far to go to get to the next one. Drop-2 voicings provide you with plenty of new neighborhoods to visit in your chord progressions.

The term "drop-2" comes from the arrangement of notes. It is an arranging technique often used for horn parts, voices, strings, etc. The tight, close-together harmonies common in horn or vocal parts are called "close voicings," which come from the closest position of the notes you can get in any chord. Here is a close position FMa7:

FIG. 16.1. FMa7 Close Position 2nd Inversion

To play that on a piano is easy. To play that on a guitar is almost impossible. Take a minute to try to reach a fingering for those notes in the order shown on the staff. The drop-2 arranging technique will help. Take the second voice (or note) from the top, or F in our example, and bring it down one octave. Here is the new arrangement of notes:

FIG. 16.2. FMa7 Drop-2 Voicing

Now go ahead and find a comfortable fingering for that. You could arrive at either of these two possibilities:

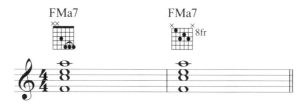

FIG. 16.3. Two FMa7 Drop-2 Fingerings

Here are three drop-2 fingerings found low on the neck as places to start; one for each adjacent string set:

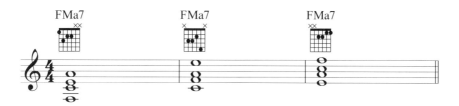

FIG. 16.4. Drop-2 FMa7 Voicings in Lowest Position

Look at the treble string form first. Identify the notes, as we've done before: E A C F. Notice that each note of the chord is on a different string; no doubles. The functions associated with those notes are 7 3 5 1. The objective now is to invert this chord to three new positions on the neck, staying with the same string set. To do this, make each chord tone move up to its next chord tone on the same string. For example, 7 moves to 1, 3 moves to 5, 5 moves to 7, and 1 moves to 3. The result:

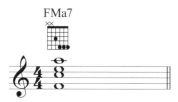

FIG. 16.5. FMa7 Drop-2 Root

The note names in order now are F C E A, or 1 5 7 3.

Continue to the next inversion the same way: 1 moves to 3, 5 moves to 7, 7 moves to 1, and 3 moves to 5. The result:

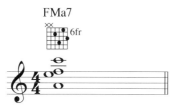

FIG. 16.6. FMa7 Drop-2 First Inversion

A E F C, or 3 7 1 5. One more time, move 3 to 5, 7 to 1, 1 to 3, and 5 to 7.

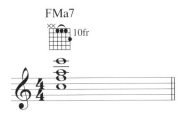

FIG. 16.7. FMa7 Drop-2 Second Inversion

C F A E or 5 1 3 7

Continue this way for the middle four strings and the four bass strings.

Figure 16.9, later in this chapter, shows the results.

Not all chords you encounter will be major 7 chords, of course. Go through each FMa7 that you have just learned and flat the 7s. You will now have twelve different ways to play F7. Go through them again and flat the 3rds to get Fmi7 twelve different ways. The chords will become most useful for you when you can use them in a sentence, as it were. The common progression II V I is an excellent way to practice memorizing these chord voicings. You'll need to transpose the chords you just found to get chords that make up II V I progressions in every key. Starting with the key of F, IImi7 is Gmi7, V7 is C7, and I is FMa7. Move the F7 that you just found up a fifth so that it becomes C7. Move the Fmi7 up a whole step to become Gmi7. Now play Gmi7 C7 FMa7 on each of the three string sets making only the smallest possible move from one chord to the next (voice lead).

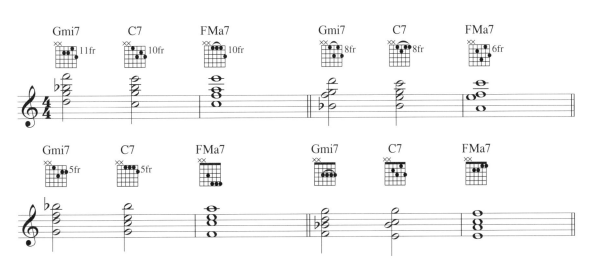

FIG. 16.8. II V I in F Drop-2 Voicings

Continue this way on the two remaining string sets.

You'll need a good shortcut to remember all of these voicings as you set out to use them in your playing. Take a moment now and circle and name the note that falls on the high E string of all of the chords on the first four strings. Is it the root, 3rd, 5th, or 7th? Now circle and name the notes on the 5th string of the chords that use the four middle strings. Similarly, identify the functions of the chord tone on that string. Finally, circle and name the notes on the low E string of the chords that use the four bass strings. Identify the function of those notes.

If you are in the area of the middle to high region of the neck and you want to grab an FMa7 chord, ask yourself: what is the 5 of the chord. The answer is C. Make the chord based around that note in the highest voice on the 8th fret of the E string. What's the 5 of a Gmi7? Make the corresponding chord that has 5 in the bass on the 5 fret of the A string, or D.

48

The results from page 53 are shown below.

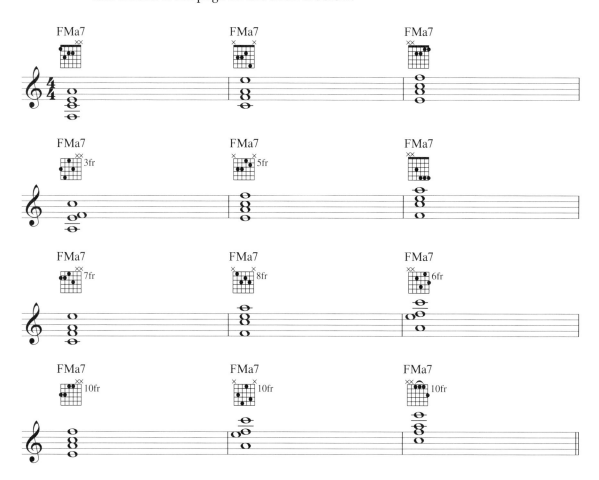

FIG. 16.9. FMa7 Drop-2 All Inversions and String Sets

CHAPTER 17

Other Chord Substitutions

There are three families of chords in a major key: tonic, subdominant, and dominant. Tonic chords are I, IIImi, and VImi. Subdominant chords are IImi and IV. The dominant chord is V. VII° (or VIImi7♭5 if we're using seventh chords) can fall into the subdominant family or the dominant family. Let's look at triads first.

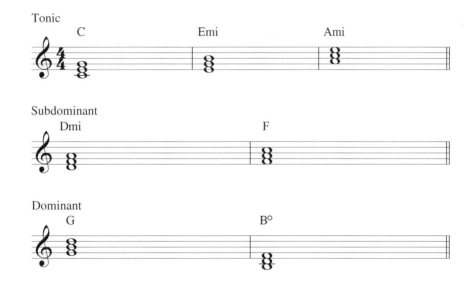

FIG. 17.1. Diatonic Triad Families

Notice the notes in common within each family. C E G, E G B, A C E. There is overlap between C and Emi and between C and Ami. D F A, F A C has overlap between the two chords. G B D can overlap with B D F. B D F can also overlap with Dmi.

These overlaps are even more obvious when we look at seventh chords.

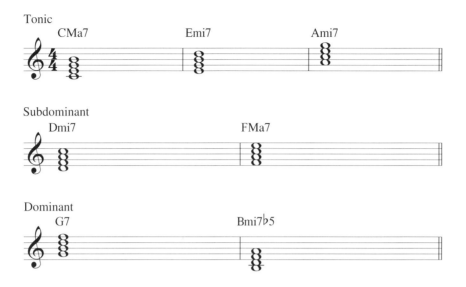

FIG. 17.2. Diatonic Seventh Chord Families

CMa7 contains an Emi triad. Ami7 contains a C major triad. Ami7 contains the first two notes of an Emi triad. In the subdominant category, Dmi7 contains an F major triad. Dominant chords, in this case G7, contain a diminished triad built on the third degree of the dominant, so B° in our example. However, that Bmi7♭5 contains a Dmi triad, along with the first two notes of an F major triad. Now we can see why the VII chord of any key plays a flexible role.

When jazz guitarists comp chords or play unaccompanied, we often substitute chords within the family of tonic, subdominant, or dominant. Play and listen to the following common chord progression:

50

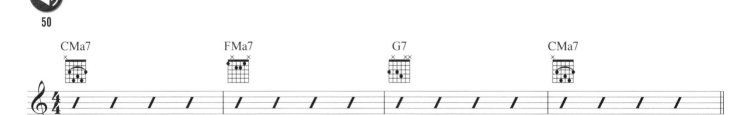

FIG. 17.3. Common Chord Progression: I IV V in C

Identify the family of each chord: CMa7 = tonic, FMa7 = subdominant, G7 = dominant. Here are some substitutions we can use based on drawing freely from the family of each chord:

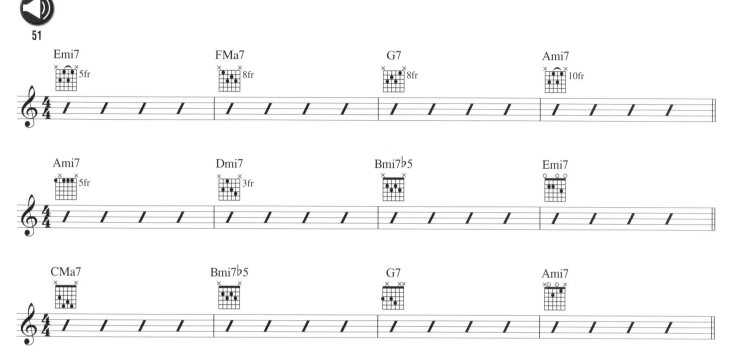

FIG. 17.4. Substitutions by Chord Families

CHAPTER 18

Diminished Chords and Scales

52

The diminished 7 chord is popularly used in jazz as a passing chord, especially between the IMa7 and the IImi7; ♯I°7 is the perfect fit there.

FIG. 18.1. Passing Diminished Example

The formula for a diminished 7 chord is 1 ♭3 ♭5 ♭♭7 (6). That's C♯, E, G and B♭ in the example above.

Diminished 7 chords are also used as a substitution for a dominant 7(♭9) chord. Take a look at the spelling of a G7(♭9): G B D F A♭. Take away the G and you're left with B°7!

Any chord tone of a diminished 7 chord can name the chord. A B°7 can also be called D°7, F°7 or A♭°7. Seen this way, a shortcut to finding the appropriate substitution for a dominant 7(♭9) chord is to go up one-half step from the root of the dominant and make the diminished 7 chord from that note. One-half step higher than G7(♭9) is A♭, so A♭°7 works. Another way to find the diminished substitution is to use any chord tone of the 7(♭9) except for the root. That is B, D, F, or A♭, but not G.

Here is a progression that uses V7(♭9) to I resolutions, followed by the same progression with diminished substitutions for the dominant chords:

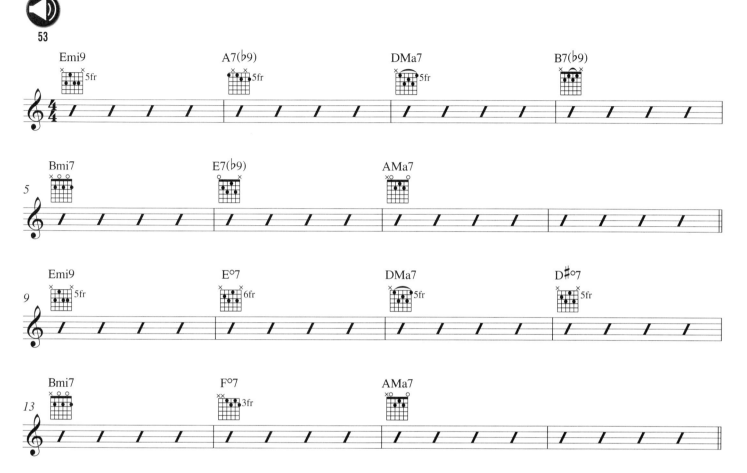

FIG. 18.2. Diminished Substitutions for Dominant Chords

Even if the chord symbol does not say ♭9 on the dominant 7 chord, if it resolves to its I chord, then you can use a diminished 7 substitution. That gives you twelve quick choices for chord voicings. Here are three forms:

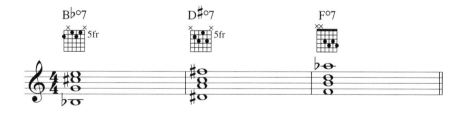

FIG. 18.3. Diminished Chord Forms

Move a diminished 7 chord three frets in either direction and you will land on the same chord. Name the notes below to see that in action:

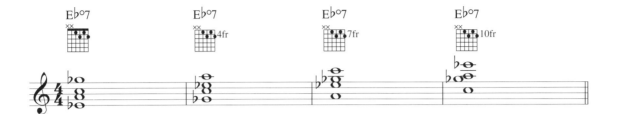

FIG. 18.4. Diminished Chord Inversions

That is an E♭°7 chord in each of those positions. It is also G♭°7, A°7, and C°7. All the same chord. Do that for each of the three diminished chord forms shown in figure 18.3, and you will have twelve ways to play the related dominant 7(♭9) chord.

A diminished scale consists of whole step, half step, whole step, half step, etc. There are only three different diminished scales, just as there are only three different diminished chords. Use E♭°7 above as a starting place. Move up one fret to get E°7, move one more fret to get F°7. One fret higher gives you G♭°7, which is the same as E♭°7, so we're back to that same chord. Diminished scales match the diminished 7 chords that way. Here is a fingering for an A diminished scale:

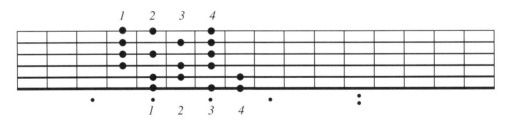

FIG. 18.5. A Diminished Scale Fingering

Since that scale matches an A°7 chord (listen to them together), and you know that an F7(♭9) can be substituted with an A°7 chord (it's one of the chord tones of the F7(♭9), you can see now that using an A diminished scale over an F7(♭9) chord will sound just right. It will pull toward the resolution to B♭Ma7, shown below.

FIG. 18.6. A Diminished Scale over F7(♭9)

The scale moves three frets in either direction just like the chords. You can start the scale on any chord tone of the dominant 7(♭9) chord except for the root. You can think up one-half step from the root of the dominant to get your starting place. Use the progressions in figure 18.2 and figure 18.6 to try out these solo ideas, and listen for the resolution as you make your way back to the major scale matching the major chord.

CHAPTER 19

Blues

The 12-bar blues is one of the most common song forms in popular music. You've heard it in early rock and roll songs like Johnny B. Goode. You've heard it in a slightly disguised form in the U2 song "I Still Haven't Found What I'm Looking For." It has been the basis for countless traditional blues songs. All of these examples use the three-chord blues form, shown in figure 19.1.

57

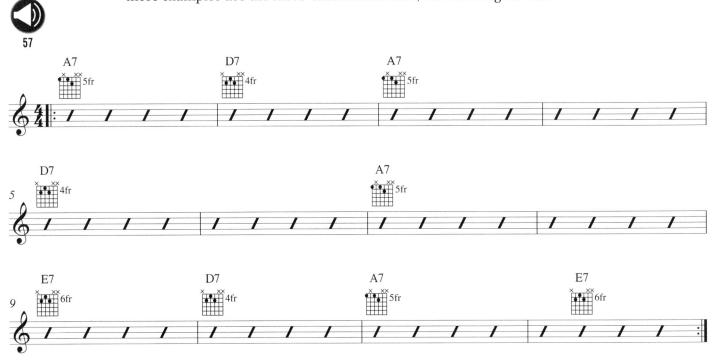

FIG. 19.1. 12-Bar Blues

Jazz blues follows the same form, but with more movement and tension added.

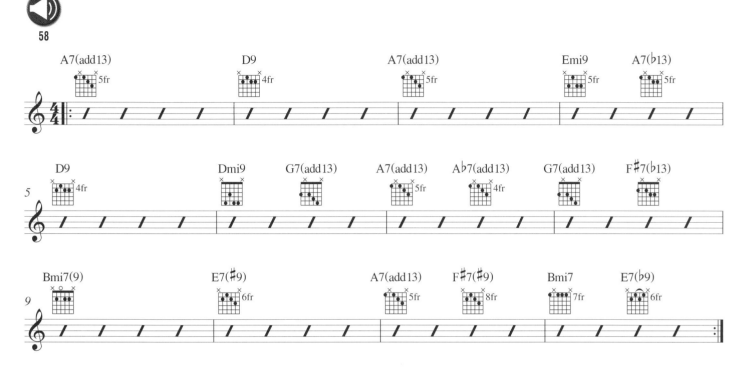

FIG. 19.2. Jazz Blues

Take a few minutes to analyze the two progressions. The three-chord blues uses I IV and V. The jazz blues uses those same chords in the right places. It is as if it is structurally intact, but with filler. Think of it as a house with all of the walls being left as is, but there is a lot of interior decorating going on. The biggest difference between the two blues progressions is in the last line. Instead of V IV I as in the three-chord blues, the jazz blues uses, not surprisingly, II V I. It's not exactly knocking a wall down; maybe more like cutting in a window.

Bar 4 uses a perfect set up to move toward the IV chord in bar 5. Alter that A7 and it will make the pull to the D7 more urgent. The Emi9 is simply the related II chord to the A7(♭13). The Dmi9 to G7(13) in bar 6 is one way to get back to the A7 in bar 7. A dominant ♭VII chord is a common chord to go back to I. Another popular way to treat bar 6 is to use the ♯IV diminished 7 chord, or D♯°7 in this case. Either way takes us back to A7 in bar 7. Look ahead to see that the first measure of the last line (bar 9) is Bmi9. What is the V7 of Bmi9? F♯7. Backtrack to see how you can get from A7(13) to F♯7(♭13) in the space of measures 7 and 8. Go chromatic! The descending root motion of A, A♭, G, F♯ is the perfect filler to get us to the set up chord of F♯7(♭13) leading to the Bmi9 in the last line. Notice that the only altered tension used in that chromatic line is the last chord. The others are moving chromatically, not in a V to I motion, so it's best to keep them natural. Finally, the turn-around in the last two bars takes you back to the top. To end, simply stay on the A7(13).

CHAPTER 20

Triads on the First Three Strings

Visualizing and playing triads all up and down the neck beginning with the first three strings can come in handy as complements to triads played in the lower position using open strings, whether you're playing solo or with another guitarist or pianist. Beyond that, they are very useful tools for improvising and comping over complex chord changes.

Here are D, F and B♭—three major triad forms that are the basis for transposing the triads themselves up the neck, and also the shapes from which the remaining three triad types (minor, diminished, and augmented) are derived. These chord forms also represent the upper structure of seventh chords, and seventh chords with tensions.

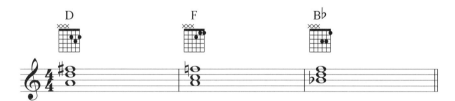

FIG. 20.1. Three Major Triad Shapes

Start by memorizing the shapes to the three triads. Our brains recognize shapes and you'll remember them more easily than trying to memorize notes right away. The D triad looks like a triangle, for example.

Consider a simple I IV V progression in G.

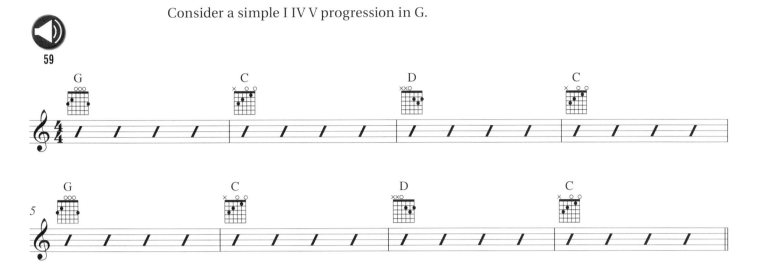

FIG. 20.2. I IV V in G

Start blocking out the triads in their new places up the neck on the first three strings. Option 1: Move that F shape up two frets, or one whole step, to land on G. Move the B♭ shape up one whole step to get C. The D can stay where it is.

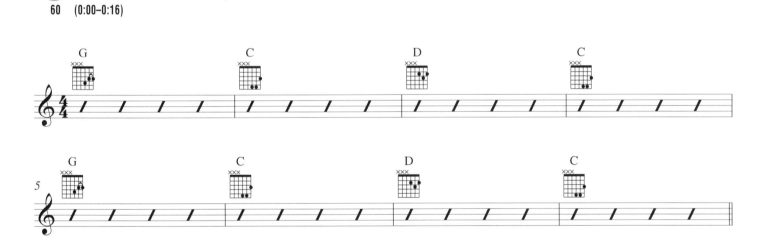

FIG. 20.3. Option 1 Movable Triads

Option 2: Move the D shape up to the 7th and 8th frets to get G. Move the F shape up to the 8th and 9th frets to get C. Move the B♭ shape up to the 5th and 7th frets to get D.

60   (0:16–0:31)

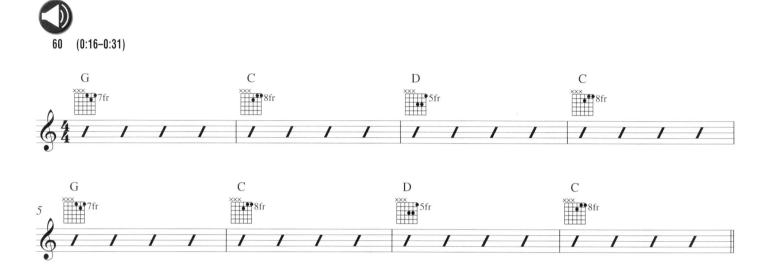

FIG. 20.4. Option 2 Movable Triads

Option 3: Move the B♭ shape up to the 10th and 12th frets to get G. Move the D shape up to the 12th and 13th frets to get C. Move the F shape up to the 10th and 11th frets to get D.

60   (0:31–0:50)

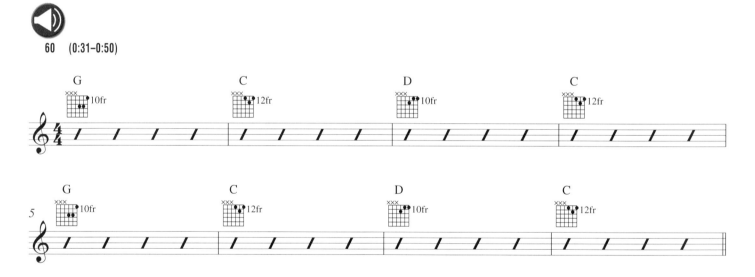

FIG. 20.5. Option 3 Movable Triads

61   62
Demo   Backing
Track Track

Play along with a friend laying down the big chords for you, or make your own backing track. Each option keeps the three triads near each other, which gives you nice smooth connections between chords, and shows possible lines to create in a melodic improvisation.

When you want a seventh chord on three strings, something has to give. It is easy to find the 7 if you know where the root is; major 7 is one fret lower than the root, ♭7 is two frets lower than the root. Look at the D major triad and its note names and functions. By moving the D on the B string down one fret, we add C♯ to the chord and now have DMa7.

FIG. 20.6. Turning D into DMa7

Here is a list of triads and seventh chords all played on the first three strings:

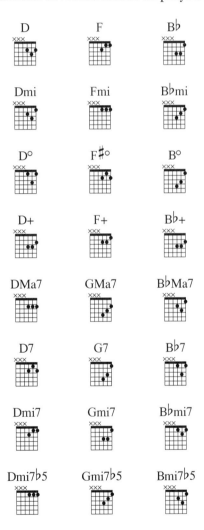

FIG. 20.7. Movable Chords on First Three Strings

You'll notice, as you move these forms around, that many chords with different names actually include the same notes: D and Bmi7, DMa7 and F♯mi, B° and G7. The upper structure of G7 is B D F, or a diminished triad. Bmi7 contains D F♯ A, or a D major triad. DMa7 contains the F♯mi triad F♯ A C♯.

To begin using these forms as improvisation tools, first block them out to memorize their positions. You should be able to go through this progression three times and play it differently each time, since there are three choices for each chord. Make sure to keep each chord as close to the chord before it as possible (voice lead).

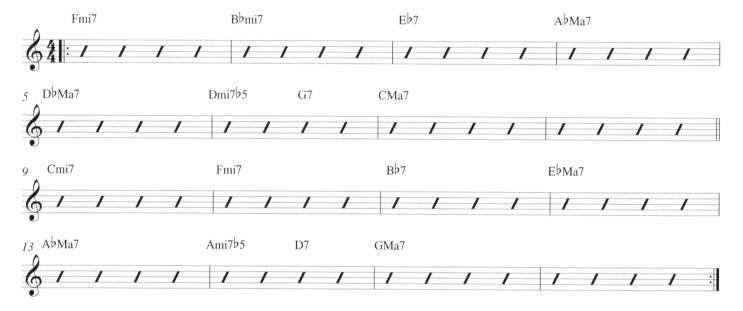

FIG. 20.8. "All the Things"

Notice that the D forms all have the third of the chord on the first string. The F and G forms have the root or the 7 on the first string, depending on whether it is a triad or a seventh chord. The B♭ and B forms all have the 5 of the chord on the first string. Get quick at identifying chord tones, and you will see right where to place these shapes on the neck. In other words, the 3 of a G chord is B. Use the D shape on the 7 fret where B will be the high note.

Once you have the triad shapes all blocked out to cover the progression, begin playing them as single note lines. They don't have to be played in any particular order, and it won't necessarily be a nice melody yet, but it will give you a good place to start in coming up with lines to play over these changes that don't stay in one key for long. Hear one example on track 65.

Now begin to branch out. You've got your places to start. You've found them near each other as you played through the progression. It's time to listen for connecting lines. Your ears will guide you through this process, along with your knowledge of scales and fingerings.

CHAPTER 21

Reading Rhythms

For those times that you're asked to sight-read a piece of music notation, I'd like you to assess the feeling in the pit of your stomach. Is it coming from having to find the notes on the neck or from having to get through the rhythms correctly? Syncopated rhythms can be especially daunting if you haven't had a chance to practice the piece and take it all apart beat by beat. Stopping to count it out is out of the question as the music blows on by. Even if you do drop out for a measure or two to work out a rhythm, it's likely you'll be too flustered to come back in and continue on to the next challenging phrase.

We learn from ear training exercises that the interval of a perfect fourth sounds like the opening to "Here Comes the Bride." A major sixth is "My Bonnie Lies Over the Ocean," and so on. A similar reference for reading rhythms follows:

67

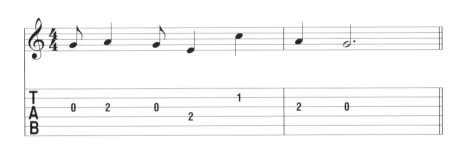

FIG. 21.1. The Rudolph Rhythm

Sound familiar yet? Try it again a couple of times, a little faster. It's Rudolph! That eighth-quarter-eighth rhythm in the beginning is "Ru-dolph the." "Red-Nosed Reindeer" is the easy part, but those first three notes are the syncopation that can be tricky to sight-read. Circle those three notes. Short long short. Da Daaa Da. If you zoom out enough when you're reading music, you'll see rhythmic passages that can be recognized this way so that you'll know what the whole phrase sounds like, rather than having to count it out one note at a time. ONE-AND two- AND… that's micro managing unnecessarily. See the bigger picture, and you'll find Rudolph rhythms are quite common.

FIG. 21.2. Rudolph Rhythm Variation

It's Rudolph Junior! Short long short. The two rhythms are the same. Play the sixteenth note rhythm at 50 bpm, and it will sound exactly like the eighth note pattern played at 100. ONE-EE-and-AH. Ru-dolph the.

It doesn't matter what the pitches are, you will at least have the rhythms down at a glance. Variations on the phrase will show up, and you will be unfazed once you see that these rests and tied notes all still conform to the Rudolph rhythm.

FIG. 21.3. More Variations on Rudolph

Shortcuts only work if they are meaningful to you. Find songs that you know well and will always remember, and relate to the rhythms this way.

In jazz and popular music, this rhythm shows up a lot:

FIG. 21.4. Common Rhythm: "Bob"

I just call it Bob. Removing the panic of counting out rhythms on the spot in favor of stepping back to see the bigger picture frees you up to concentrate on finding the notes on the neck.

Name That Chord 1

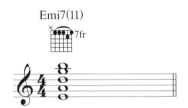

FIG. 22.1. Name This Chord

First, as always, name the notes. Open E can be your bass note for now, then the 7th fret on the A string is E, 7th fret on D is A, 7th fret on G is D, 8th fret on B is G, and 7th fret on E is B. The chord consists of: E A D G B. If E is the root, you need to figure out what the other notes are in relation to E. You'll see 1 (root), 4 or 11, ♭7, ♭3, and 5. Unscramble those numbers to get 1, ♭3, 5, ♭7, and 11. There's a clear vision of an Emi7 chord with an 11 added, or Emi7(11). Sometimes you'll see this chord more informally called Emi11. It's best to be more specific so there's no doubt about the presence or absence of a 9. When you first identify the notes and their functions, don't make a judgment as to whether the A is going to be a 4 or an 11. You have to see the whole picture before you can determine that in fact there is a 3 in there as well as a 7, so the A is not functioning as a sus4, and it is in fact being added to a minor 7 chord, deeming it to be the tension above the 7, or 11. Take it for a little ride. It sounds nice going to A7 then DMa7—a typical II V I.

Suppose now that the bass player gives you an A below that chord. Erase the labels you had given those notes, and reassign them to new roles. Leave off the low open E string this time to be clear that A has the bottom end. The note names remain the same: E A D G B. So, as related to A, E = 5, A = 1, D = 4 or 11, G = ♭7, and B = 2 or 9. This time, there's no 3, so the D is functioning as the sus4. You have, in order, 1 4 5 ♭7 9. That's an A9(sus4). Try it out by tapping your 5th fret on the 6th string followed by strumming this A9(sus4). It's a nice open sound that you can use in place of any other A7(sus4) you might be familiar with. It doesn't necessarily have to resolve to an A9; it can move freely to another chord, or resolve to a D of some sort. This chord has a lot of possibilities in its role in a progression and in the mood that it creates.

What if the bass player gives you a D? 2 or 9, 5, 1, 4 or 11, 6 or 13. D6(9)sus4? It could happen. It might be just the thing as part of a chord melody solo or a delayed resolution to a D6(9).

What if the bass player gives you a G? 6 or 13, 9, 5, 1, 3. That's a little more reasonable and a reliable choice for a G6(9) if you choose. See how you like it in context: Ami7 to D7 to G6(9).

Now the bass player is giving you a B. You get 4 or 11, ♭7, ♭3, ♭6 or ♯5 or ♭13, and 1. Bmi7♯5(11). This is a nice, rich chord that may or may not want to resolve back to a natural 5 in its travels. See how you like it going to a CMa7 or even a CMa7(♯11). That would imply the III and IV chords in the key of G.

There are no more chord tones for that bass player to provide, but try a C in the bass. 3, 6 or 13, 2 or 9, 5, and 7. Assembling them in order shows us 3 5 7 9 13. It's a CMa7(9,13). Again, be careful not to call it a CMa13, just to clarify the absence of the 11 in there. (If you give players who are reading your charts every advantage with clear chord symbols, there will be fewer questions and a stronger likelihood that your parts will be played just as you originally heard them in your mind's ear).

Play an F in the bass. You now have 7, 3, 6 or 13, 9, and ♯11. 3 7 9 ♯11 13. It's an FMa13. Still, be safe and say FMa9(♯11,13). Notice that the 5 of the chord is not there, and also notice that it is not missed. The chord is a gorgeous zinger of an ending. Play Gmi7 C7 FMa9(♯11,13). That ♯11 on top as a high note will grab your listener's ear. It is so full of color and tension that it even makes a pretty cool ending to a blues in F, major 7 and all. Try it out in the beginning and middle of songs, too.

You can experiment with other notes in the chromatic scale functioning as the bass against this voicing. It's a workout trying to name some of them, and they will not often stay in your vocabulary, but it's fun to see anyway. When all else fails, and before you get too stressed, remember that you can always say Emi7(11)/A♭.

CHAPTER 23

Name That Chord 2

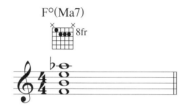

FIG. 23.1. Name This Chord 2

What would you like to call it? First, name those notes: F B E A♭. Or, enharmonically: F C♭ E G♯. Or: F B E G♯. Now, you can see an E triad in the second inversion at the end. You might have recognized it by the shape already, with its familiar three in a row across the 9th fret. You can call it E/F, or an E triad with F in the bass. Call it F C♭ E A♭ for a different perspective. There is an F diminished triad in there: F A♭ C♭ (also known as B). The E natural makes it an F diminished major seven, or F°Ma7. Put a bossa nova groove to Gmi7 C7 and then go to F°Ma7 before resolving to FMa7. That's that beautiful delayed resolution that you hear in bossas and other jazz contexts.

71

FIG. 23.2. II V I with Delayed Resolution

What else could you call it? Think outside of the notes that are there and think in the context of an assumed root. What if D♭ is the root? Now you have the 3 (F) the ♭7 (B) the ♯9 (E) and the 5 (A♭). That's a D♭7(♯9).

Make G the root this time. You'll see the ♭7 (F) the 3 (B) the 13 (E) and the ♭9 (A♭). It's a G7(♭9,13). That's a mixed bag that contains an altered tension and a natural tension.

Notice that the F, or the lowest note in that chord is the 3 of the D♭7 chord. That means that when you want any 7(♯9) chord, put the 3 on the A string, make the triad shape on the next fret, and you've got a ♯9 chord. Try it out with the more familiar Hendrix version of a dominant 7(♯9).

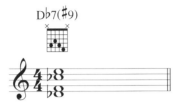

FIG. 23.3. Common 7(♯9) Voicing

You'll hear that they are the same chord.

On the other hand, if you think of F as the ♭7 of G7, then you can use that to find any dominant 7(♭9,13) chord. Go to the flat 7 of any chord, put that on the A string, and make the triad shape on the next fret to play a dominant 7(♭9,13) chord.

The best part is hearing those dominant chords resolve to their I chord. If G is V, what's I? C. So, play that 7th and 8th fret version of the chord form to get G7(♭9,13). Follow that with a CMa9.

Think of it as a D♭7(♯9) and follow that with its I chord, which is G♭.

If you add this one easy-to-make chord to your chord collection, you will have a few different ways to use it. Be on the lookout for opportunities as you comp through some standard tunes. Be ready for a delayed resolution to throw in, as in F°Ma7, or a dominant 7(♯9) going to I major or I minor as in D♭7(♯9), or a dominant 7(♭9,13) going to I major or I minor, as in G7(♭9,13). Transpose all over the neck for best results.

CHAPTER 24

Ear Training

You don't have to have perfect pitch to have good ears. You can develop great ears by memorizing the syllables of the major scale. If you can sing the scale forward and backward using the syllables of the scale: Do Re Mi Fa Sol La Ti Do, you're off to a good start.

Improvising is essential to jazz. Ear training is essential to improvising. *Solfege* is essential to ear training. Solfege is the practice of singing the syllables of the scale within a key, matching the written note to the correct syllable of the scale. The third degree of a major scale is Mi, the sixth degree is La, and so on.

Here are some phrases to use as practice for solfege. Sing them without your guitar in your hands first. You don't have to actually be a singer to do this. You just want to develop the pitch recognition. Matching the pitches and intervals to the syllables will have you transcribing and identifying scale degrees and chord tones easily.

72   (0:00–0:48)

FIG. 24.1. Solfege Practice

C is "Do," or the root of the key, in these examples. Most of the phrases started and ended on notes other than C. When you sing the syllables rather than the note names, you are memorizing the relationship between Do and all of the other pitches. That relationship works in any key.

Try these in the key of F:

72   (0:50–1:38)

FIG. 24.2. Solfege Practice in F

The melodies are the same as in figure 24.1; the syllables should be the same, even though the note names have changed. Go ahead and play both examples on the guitar.

73

Listen to the following chords on the recording:

FMa7   **B♭mi7**   **Dmi7♭5**   **C9**   **Gmi9**   **C6**

Notation here has been intentionally left out. Identify the highest note of each chord by listening to it. The root of the chord can function as Do. Is the highest note Sol? Mi? Do? Is it a chord tone or not? Can you get it by singing up from Do, or singing back from Do? Can you get it from making a leap from Do without singing the pitches in between? Once you have identified the pitch by its syllable, you can name the note by applying your knowledge of theory (i.e. Sol is 5, if Do is A♭, 5 is E♭).

Melodies (and therefore improvised lines) skip around, of course, so it's a good idea to practice solfege that skips around as well. An easy way to begin is with chord tones, as shown here:

FIG. 24.3. Solfege Practice with Chord Tones

Keep C in your mind's ear as Do, and relate everything else to that.

Try these more random skips:

FIG. 24.4. Solfege Practice with Random Skips

Take some time right now to improvise over a familiar progression, like I VI II V. As you play, be aware of the syllable of your starting note of each phrase. On what pitch would you like to end your phrase? Hear it and play it. Create a line within the major scale that runs up and down a few notes repeatedly. Sing the syllables. Is it memorable? Can you repeat it easily? Skip around some. Can you land on a note that you hear in your mind's ear by matching the syllable with its right place in the scale?

Ear training can continue throughout your day. Whenever and wherever you find yourself listening to music, see if you can identify the root motion, or the bass notes of the chord progression. You don't have to know the name of the key, just hear Do and relate everything else to that. Listen to a lyric in a song and identify the pitch that the word "love" lands on. Listen to a guitar solo (or a sax or piano solo), and choose a note at the beginning or end of a phrase to identify. Listen for a three- or four-note phrase, as we did above, and find the syllables to match.

CHAPTER 25

Comping

Comping is the art of supporting a melody. "Comp" comes from the word "accompaniment." The function of chords is supporting a melody. A very effective way to comp is to listen to the highest voice in each chord. Make the change to the next chord create a logical melody line if the high note were singled out. Think of this as melody with a small "m." We are still in the supportive role behind the Melody with a capitol "M." The Melody should be the standout prominent voice. The melody that rides around on top of the harmony should be interesting but respectful. Chords that leap all around the neck without regard to easy connections can be very distracting, as well as a lot of work for your fretting hand. The solution is to collect as many chord forms as you can throughout your guitar playing life. In addition to that collection of chords, you will find that when you add fretted notes for the sake of their melodic connections from one chord to the next, you will be finding and creating new chord voicings on the spot.

Consider the following simple chord progression in the key of C.

FIG. 25.1. I II III IV in C

You might be able to find a few different ways to play those chords right away. As you do, listen to the highest note of each chord. Can you single those notes out as you play? Do they make a memorable melody line? (small "m" here; there's no Melody yet). What if you decide which strings to play and which string to leave out? Get your picking hand involved in the process. The chord forms shown on the next page illustrate one possibility for comping that line.

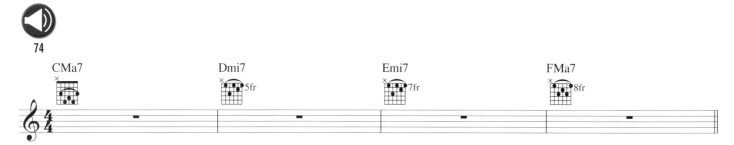

FIG. 25.2. Chord Forms

Now make a couple of adjustments. Stop at the second string of the CMa7 chord, making the note "E" the highest one you hear. Before moving on to Dmi7, move your fourth finger up to the 6th fret so you hear the note "F." Now rearrange your fingers to make Dmi7 become the more colorful Dmi7(add11).

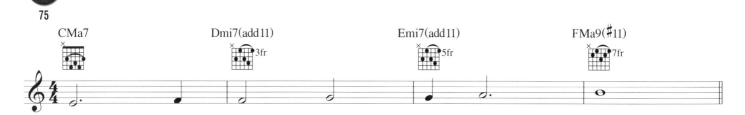

FIG. 25.3. Adding Melody to Chords

The "G" on the first string is a follow up from the "E" and "F" of the CMa7 chord that came before.

Play the Emi7 as shown, resulting in Emi7(11) so that we can accommodate the melody "G" on the B string and "A" on the E string.

Finally, land on FMa9(♯11). Go ahead and play all the way to the first string to hear that nice "B" natural in the highest voice.

Let's look at the resulting melody by itself:

FIG. 25.4. Melody from Chord Voicings

You've stayed true to the original chord progression without even using any notes outside of the key of C. You've created a flow of chords that would provide a nice supportive role behind a Melody. You've moved gradually up the neck without any awkward leaps and bounds. You've made sense of your choices of strings to play with your picking hand, whether you play pick style or finger style.

Challenge yourself to find ways to connect your chords smoothly and creatively behind a melody player or singer. You'll want to make sure that your choice of voicings and resulting melody lines work well with the Melody.

CHAPTER 26

Bass Lines

Guitarists, like pianists, can play accompaniment roles or melody roles. One very effective way to comp in jazz is simply a single-note bass line. You'll hear guitarists doing this in duo contexts with other guitarists or pianists. A simple quarter-note bass line makes a swing feel without clutter or distraction.

In 4/4 time, a typical walking bass line will take up four beats in each measure. If there is just one chord in the measure, start on the root and then use the next likely strong bass note—the 5—on beat 3, that only leaves two beats to fill. Make one of those an approach note to the target chord root of the next measure, and that leaves a total of one beat to be as creative as you want! Notice in the example below how often the approach note is one-half step below or above the target note, which is the root of the chord in the next measure.

77
"Leaves"

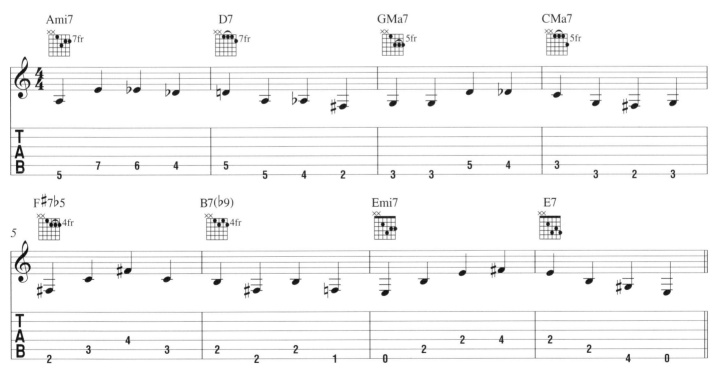

FIG. 26.1. Chords and Bass

Another way to create a bass line is to use scale steps rather than only chord tones or approaches. There will still be room for creativity and approach notes, as you can see in the example below.

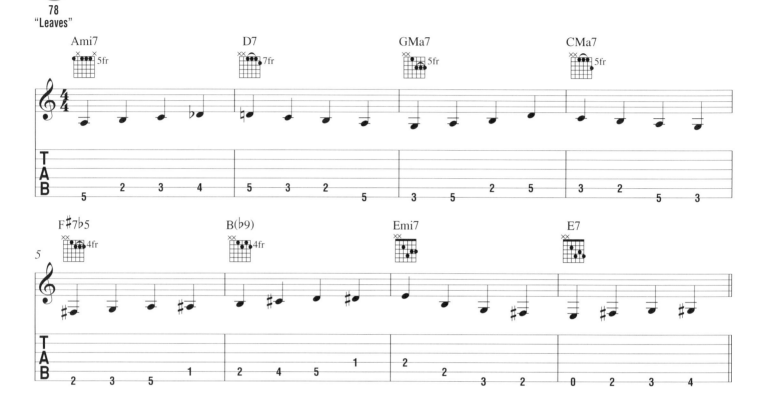

FIG. 26.2. Bass Line to "Leaves"

Make a backing track for yourself that only consists of bass lines, or use the one provided. Improvise over the line, and judge for yourself if the chords are outlined or stated enough for you. Listen to bass players intently after you've practiced these lines and ideas. You will begin to tune in to the ways in which a chord progression can be expressed through the single line alone. Listen to guitarists and pianists accompany each other; I suggest the Bill Evans and Jim Hall album *Undercurrent* (Poll Winners, 2013) to hear how masterfully it can be done.

CHAPTER 27

Melody Awareness

When someone asks you to play something, what do you play? Many of you will remember the experience of feeling so excited to have learned "a song." You can get a lot of mileage out of a handful of chords. But, oh, the missing melody. It plagues guitar players.

Choose a song to which you know the chords down cold. Have the melody in your head. Are any of those melody notes near the chords the way you have them fingered? If not, can you rearrange things so that you can reach a melody note where and when you want to? Go ahead, and let go of the chord all together if you need to in order to reach the melody. Play the melody as a single note line to locate all of the notes, whether you can read the notation or you're just finding them by ear. In other words, make the melody the top priority when you're playing guitar. Even if you're a singer, you're going to want to take an instrumental solo break now and then. Feel that freedom of letting go of the chord. It's okay. You can get it back. You can play the bass note of the next chord if you want. Just try letting go. Just for now. Melody Awareness achieved!

Keep your attention on the melody as you play the following example:

FIG. 27.1. Chord Melody in G

CHAPTER 28

Dynamics

Whether you play pick style or finger style, dynamics play an important role in the presentation of a performance piece. Consider some real-life examples. You have a teacher (or a boss or a parent or a spouse…) who talks at you in long-winded bouts of loudness, and possibly all on the same pitch. You stop paying any attention to what they're saying, in favor of scanning the room looking for the exits. Your head turns away a little to protect your ears. Now, if I sit forward in my chair a bit and lean in your direction saying, "Hey," glancing around, "I've gotta tell you something," in a whisper meant just for you, you'll lean in, too, eager to hang on the next words. Anyone else in earshot will perk up their ears, too. It's irresistible. It's the old saying at work, "If you want to get someone's attention, whisper."

Loudness has its place, to be sure. We have the whole spectrum of soft to loud as a tool for expressing our arrangements and performances.

For finger-style players: start with your third finger on the first string, open E. Play as quietly as you possibly can; don't let anyone hear you. Stay with that one finger and increase the volume very gradually, trying to remain in control of the crescendo. When you are playing as loudly as you can with that one finger on that one string, take it back down to zero just as gradually. Repeat with each finger (second finger on the open B string and first finger on the open G string). Now repeat the exercise with your thumb on each bass string (D, A, and E). Go through the whole process again, but this time use fretted notes on each string. Be as creative as you want here; the note choices are up to you. It's all about the picking hand. Put your awareness on the feeling of each string. Hear and feel the differences between the open strings and the fretted notes, the treble strings and the bass strings. You will also feel and hear a difference between your thumb and your fingers. Your thumb will be naturally louder, moving in a downward direction with more power than your three fingers closing in toward your palm. Try playing both open E strings together at the same volume using your thumb and third finger. Now try fretted notes on those strings. Now try eighth notes on the low E and quarter notes on the high E. Which is louder? Again, play your extreme crescendo.

Pick-style players can do the same exercise one string at a time, open strings and then fretted notes. It is not a speed drill, but rather a listening exercise and a chance to feel the range of volume that you and your guitar are capable of using.

Next, pick a tune that you like to play. A standard tune, a blues, a pop song, your choice. Play the first line very softly. Play the second line very loudly. Play the next line at a medium volume. Do this with the chords and the melody. Now make your own choices as to when to rise and fall dynamically with the melody. There will be a natural flow to the expression of the tune that you will begin to feel. If there are dynamic markings on a page you are reading, ignore them for now. Use your ears and your instinct to create your own dynamic arrangement. Finally, listen to recordings of your favorite pieces and your favorite players. Listen solely for the dynamic expressions in their playing. Is there anything that you would do differently? Make a mental note of that.

By the way, this is a good exercise to try in conversation with people, too: as a listener and a speaker.

CHAPTER 29

Chord Solos

Solo jazz guitarists play songs all by themselves including the melody and chords played together along with a groove of some sort, whether it is a swing feel with a walking bass line, a straight-eighth Latin feel, or a ballad played rubato. For performing singer-songwriters who want to have something interesting to play between verses or during an instrumental break, learning chord solos can make the difference between an adequate performance and a sparkling arrangement well played. Start with something simple to get a feel for the concept, and then you'll be able to move confidently toward creating your own chord solo arrangements of jazz standards—even on sight! That skill will transfer easily to adding melodies to your accompaniment parts that you already know, whether you're playing original songs or familiar tunes of others.

The hymn "We Gather Together" is a good place to start to understand the process of mixing melodies and chords together on the guitar. The strategy is to keep the melody note the highest note in the chord. Listeners' ears will perceive the highest note as the melody when played this way.

Play the chord on beat 1 of each measure, or at the point of the chord change if there is more than one chord per bar. Keep a simple strum that goes from the bass note to the melody note. Play the remaining melody notes as a single line, but hold the chord down with your fretting hand for as long as you can. Sometimes, the melody note won't be in the chord naturally, so you'll have to add it, like the D in the melody as we first play the G chord in bar 1. The D is a chord tone, but you might not have voiced the chord with the D on top normally.

C

We Gather Together

16th Century Dutch
Arranged by Jane Miller

FIG. 29.1. "We Gather Together" Chord Solo

Next, add some filler. The long melody notes give you some time to add other notes from the chord either in a finger-style arpeggio, or as a pick-style strumming. Bars 17–32 show some filler examples. When you're comfortable with this hymn, use the same process while going through lead sheets of some jazz standards. Find a way to make the melody note stay on top of your chord voicing, even if it is not a chord tone. Here is one that I've written to show that even non-chord tones can be incorporated into the voicings.

83

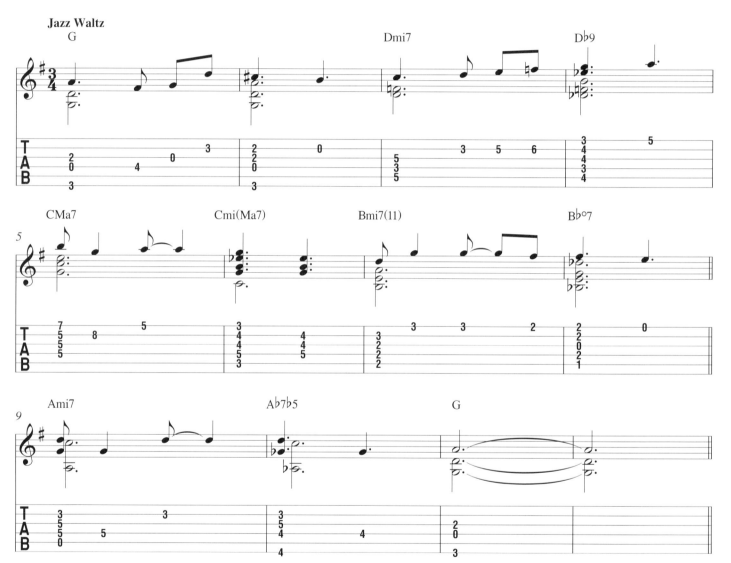

FIG. 29.2. Chord Solo in G

CHAPTER 30

Pentatonic Scales

Many guitarists learned to play a pentatonic scale before playing anything else. It is a five-note scale that comes from the major scale that shares its name. When the entire major scale seems too pretty or too much, try a pentatonic scale. Remove the half-steps from the major scale and you will have it. Think: 1 2 3 5 6.

84   (0:00–0:08)

FIG. 30.1. C Major Pentatonic Scale

The opening riff to "My Girl" uses the notes in a major pentatonic scale. Start with your fourth finger on the note C to hear the major pentatonic sound. Shift the tonal center to A and you will hear the relative minor of the C major pentatonic, or A minor pentatonic.

84   (0:09–0:15)

FIG. 30.2. Relative Minor Pentatonic Scale

85
Demo
Track

86
Backing
Track

Use a C major pentatonic in the key of C, of course. Try it out against a I VI
II V, or CMa7 Ami7 Dmi7 G7.

87
Demo
Track

88
Backing
Track

Think of the relative minor key to use the scale in that context. Use typical
chords in A minor: Ami7 Dmi7 Emi7.

89
Demo
Track

90
Backing
Track

The relative minor works beautifully in a blues. Use A minor for an A blues:

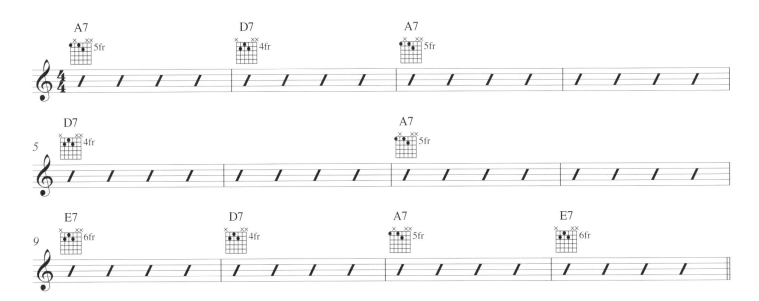

FIG. 30.3. A Blues

91

Add blue notes to the scale by adding the flat 5, or E♭ in this example.

FIG. 30.4. A Blues Scale

Now record yourself playing this D9 chord.

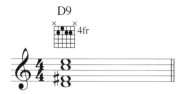

FIG. 30.5. D9

Listen to the A minor pentatonic scale over that chord. This is especially cool if the D9 is extended over several bars. It helps for transposing purposes if you think of the scale as the related II of the V chord, which is the dominant chord. Ami7 to D9 makes a II V progression, so use the A minor scale with the D9 chord.

Here is another fingering for the A minor pentatonic scale, which can be transposed the same way that you would transpose any scale. Think of this fingering as starting on the 5 of the minor scale, or the 3 of the major scale.

84 (0:16–0:24)

FIG. 30.6. A Minor Pentatonic from 5

CHAPTER 31

Think Small

Improvising comes from every possibility imaginable. Even while playing the simplest of tonal music with the intention of being dedicated to playing over the changes, you're met with an overwhelming amount of choices to make. If you set some limitations on a practice session, you'll open a door to creativity within those parameters. You'll have some puzzles to solve; you'll have to figure out how to get from here to there without going out of bounds. Start with a familiar diatonic progression:

CMa7   **Ami7**   **Dmi7**   **G7**

Make yourself a backing track. Keep it simple, but make it long. Now improvise a line that stays diatonic to C but only uses the interval of thirds—major or minor. That's the only limit for now. Your choice of strings, fret positions, melody shape. Try to move beyond the more typical scale practice that you probably already do and come up with a melody based on thirds. You can use a variety of rhythms. You can leave space. All the notes played have to move in thirds, that's all.

Now, try fourths. Keep it diatonic, so some will be tritones.

Stay with fourths but play only on adjacent strings within each phrase.

Now play any diatonic note you want, but always skip a string between notes, either ascending or descending.

Now, only play on the third and fourth strings.

Now, only play on the first two strings in the 5th fret position.

You will want to make up your own limits and play these puzzle-solving games in different keys. In the process, you will be getting at some useful information and ideas that you would not have stumbled upon otherwise.

CHAPTER 32

Memorizing Tunes, Rhythm Changes, and AABA Form

Collecting memorized tunes is important to a performing jazz player. If you made a list right now, how many songs would you include that you have memorized? In fact, make three lists: one for memorized melodies (or "heads"), one for chords, and ones that you can play by yourself in chord-melody style. These are the three roles jazz guitarists play. To learn standard tunes, listen to the great singers of the standards: Ella Fitzgerald, Tony Bennett, Sarah Vaughan, and Billie Holiday. Learn the forms in your head. Listen for the verses and the bridges. Listen to the singer's interpretation of the music—the way they take liberties rhythmically, the way they embellish the melody. Know the tunes the way you would know the latest pop song if it came on in a store. Be able to sing along. You've seen the benefit of knowing a song in your head before you set out to read it (the Rudolph rhythm…).

When you are on a bandstand with other musicians and a tune gets called that you might not have played before, it will help if you've at least heard the tune as played by others. Sure, you'll probably be able to read a chord chart on the spot, but once you memorize a tune, you will be able to say so much more about it in your playing.

Understanding and feeling forms is a good first step toward memorizing a tune. You will at least know the structure of the song, and you will be confident when it's time to go to the bridge. Here is an AABA song form:

AABAAABAAABAAABAAABAAABAAABAAABAAABAAABA

It is a very familiar song form, but seen this way, you can understand how easy it can be to become lost. Most AABA forms have eight bars per section. Something happens, then it happens again. Then something different happens, then the first thing that happened happens again. That's the form. The song "Yesterday" is a famous example of an AABA song form. Oddly, the A sections are seven bars each, yet we know the song so well that it flows effortlessly by.

Another well-known AABA song form is Gershwin's "I Got Rhythm." Each section is eight bars long. Many jazz tunes have been written using the same chords to that song; so much so that those chord changes have become known as "Rhythm Changes," short for "I Got Rhythm." "Oleo," by Sonny Rollins is an example of a song based on rhythm changes. Originally, the song "I Got Rhythm" had a melody written for the bridge. Over time, jazz players left the bridge to be improvised during the heads. Here are rhythm changes in C:

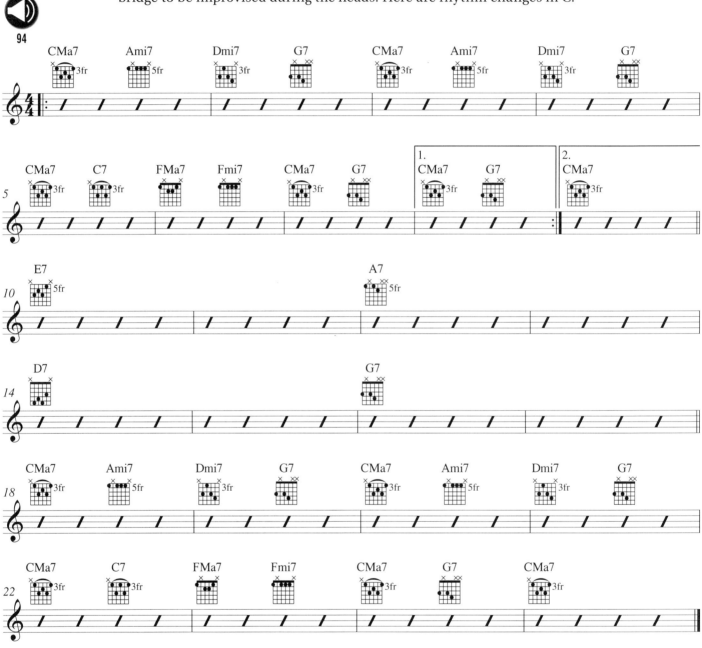

FIG. 32.1. "Rhythm Changes" in C

Hum the melody, or any melody you choose for this chord progression. Play the chords only, but keep the melody in your mind's ear. Be the one in the band who knows when it's time to go to the bridge. Once you're comfortable with these changes, try the modified version below.

95
Demo
Track

96
Backing
Track

FIG. 32.2. Reharmonized "Rhythm Changes"

It's even more important to hold onto a melody while playing these chords behind a soloist so that you will always know your place in the form. Good drummers will punctuate the phrases for you, outlining the eight-bar sections with accents or fills.

Someone will definitely call "Rhythm Changes" on your gig or at your jam session. Memorize this form, the original chords, and the reharmonized chords so that you will be completely comfortable playing behind anyone. If you make a backing track for yourself, practice soloing and get comfortable with that aspect, too. These changes have a little bit of everything to offer from what you've been practicing in this book. By learning this one AABA song form down cold, other AABA song forms will be easy to grasp. You will be the one in the band who knows when to go to the bridge.

AFTERWORD

I have a pretty respectable record collection that still resides in the bottom shelves of a couple of large bookcases. The records represent a history of popular music and jazz, along with a smattering of chamber music and whatnot. They also represent my musical development. Listening to singer-songwriters who could really play guitar, like Janis Ian and Kenny Rankin, made me trace back their history to Billie Holiday and Antonio Carlos Jobim. That led to checking out Barney Kessel and João Gilberto. Before too long, I was bringing home and devouring Ella Fitzgerald records with Joe Pass, and grabbing anything I could find by Wes Montgomery. I learned standard tunes as sung by Ella, Billie, Sarah Vaughan, Betty Carter, Tony Bennett, Eddie Jefferson, Anita O'Day, and Lambert, Hendricks, and Ross. It didn't matter if there was a guitar player on the recordings or not; I was memorizing the music by listening to the great singers and instrumentalists. It's a folk tradition, really. Songs get passed on, shared, recorded. Indeed, jazz soloists are great storytellers in their improvisations. Once you know the music in your head, your mind's ear, your heart, and your bones, you will get the little jokes that are told through the musical phrases. As you set out now to create your own musical stories, your own jokes will get better and better, too.

97
"The Great Above"

ABOUT THE AUTHOR

Photo by Emily Joy Ashman

Jane Miller is a guitarist, composer, and arranger with roots in both jazz and contemporary acoustic guitar worlds. She is a featured guitarist in noted jazz journalist Scott Yanow's 2013 book *The Great Jazz Guitarists: A Complete Guide.* The Jane Miller Group has released three CDs. Her fourth CD, her first solo guitar recording called *Three Sides to a Story,* was released in June 2013.

Jane has performed solo and in duo and group settings around the United States. In addition to leading her own jazz instrumental quartet, she is in a working chamber jazz trio with saxophonist Cercie Miller and bassist David Clark, for which she contributes many compositions. She has been a guest guitarist with SONiA, of *disappear fear,* traveling and recording with the internationally acclaimed singer-songwriter.

Jane is a contributing editor to *Acoustic Guitar Magazine,* and is a former monthly columnist for *Premier Guitar Magazine.* She has also written for Mel Bay publishing company's online magazine, *Guitar Sessions,* and the Berklee guitar department magazine, *Open Position.*

Jane joined the guitar department faculty at Berklee College of Music in 1994, where she is a professor. She has contributed arrangements for solo guitar to the guitar department library, and has performed solo recitals and concerts with her group in the Berklee Performance Center and recital halls.

Jane is a jazz guitar instructor for jamplay.com, for whom she has recorded over 65 video lessons and does live on-camera chats for students from around the world each week. For more information about Jane Miller and her music, please visit janemillergroup.com.

INDEX

Guitar Books and Videos
from Berklee Press